Essential
Seychelles

by

CHRISTINE OSBORNE

Christine Osborne is a travel writer with a
special interest in the East. She has travelled
widely in the Middle East, North Africa and
Southeast Asia. Among the books she has
written are *Essential Thailand* and
Essential Bali and Jakarta in this series.
Christine is also a professional photographer,
and took most of the photographs in this book.

AA

Produced by AA Publishing

Written by Christine Osborne
Peace and Quiet section
by Paul Sterry
Series Adviser: Ingrid Morgan
Series Controller: Nia Williams
Copy Editor: Audrey Horne

Edited, designed and produced by
AA Publishing. Maps © The
Automobile Association 1992.

Distributed in the United Kingdom
by AA Publishing, Fanum House,
Basingstoke, Hampshire, RG21 2EA.

A CIP catalogue record for this
book is available from the British
Library.

ISBN 0 7495 0318 1

Published by The Automobile
Association.

Typesetting: Avonset, Midsomer
Norton, Bath.
Colour separation: L.C. Repro,
Aldermaston

Printed in Italy by Printers S.R.L.,
Trento

Front cover picture: Beach on Mahé

Author's Acknowledgements

The author would like to thank the following people and organisations for their help in
researching this guide:
Air Seychelles, Seychelles Tourist Office (Victoria), Marie-Nella Deller and Liz Naya of
the Seychelles Tourist Office (London), Denis Island, Bird Island and Ornella La Polla of
Silhouette.
Howard Mason of Travel Services Seychelles, Mason's Travel, National Travel and Len
Mole of the Royal Society in London.
The Sunset Beach Hotel, Paradise Resorts and Michael Hoireau of Seychelles Hotels.
The author is especially grateful to Judy Greeven, Public Relations (Seychelles) London.

This book employs a
simple rating system to
help choose which
places to visit:

◆◆◆   do not miss

◆◆   see if you can

◆   worth seeing if
you have time

INTRODUCTION

The late Archbishop Makarios of Cyprus, on leaving Seychelles in 1957, after exile there, wrote: '. . . It is no exaggeration to say the Seychelles islands contain the most beautiful places I have ever seen. I do not like to question General Gordon's belief that it is the biblical Garden of Eden, but it is certainly a place which is entitled, by its very nature, to have this name . . .'

Veteran travellers agree that Seychelles is a winner, and not only in the beauty stakes. It is an ideal haven for the refugee from crowded, polluted city life. Swaying palms and white sand beaches washed by a turquoise ocean is a typical brochure picture of Seychelles. There are scores of islands like this in the archipelago. The tropical climate means constant warm temperatures; the flora and fauna are curious and often unique; there are fine hotels and a variety of watersports – and some of the friendliest people on earth. Seychelles is a place of superlatives. It has, in

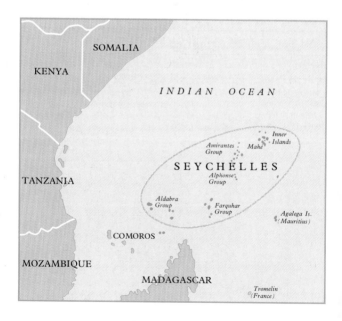

Anse Sévère at the northeastern tip of La Digue offers a typical picture of an island paradise

Aldabra Atoll, the world's largest coral atoll; in the giant tortoise of Aldabra, the world's largest land tortoise; and in the coco-de-mer of Praslin, perhaps the world's most erotic plant. Its male and female fruits are said to couple after dark in the Vallée de Mai, where the palms grow wild.

Of the 115 or so Seychelles islands, only a few are linked by good sea and air connections giving easy access to visitors. Each one has its own character and interest.

Mahé, the largest island, is by far the most developed and visited, yet its mountainous interior remains largely untrodden.

Silhouette, like Mahé a lush, granitic island and only an hour and a half away by boat, preserves a lifestyle little changed since the last century. Out in the ocean to the north of the main island group are the beautiful coral islands of Bird (Île aux Vaches), with its colony of sooty terns, and Denis, famous for fishing.

Also for bird-lovers are the islands of Frégate and La Digue, refuges for two of the world's rarest birds – the Seychelles magpie robin and the Seychelles black paradise flycatcher. Adventure and romance are also found in the island paradise. There are tales of hidden treasure, particularly that of the pirate 'La Buse', believed to be buried at Bel Ombre on Mahé's west coast. As for romance... more and more couples are choosing to marry in Seychelles. Travel agents offer special wedding packages, and honeymooners abound.

Add the casual lifestyle and the absence of violent crime to these attractions and Seychelles comes out top of the list of tropical holiday destinations. Advance reservations are essential, as the government limits visitors to 4,000 at any one time, a wise move to ensure 'paradise' is not spoilt.

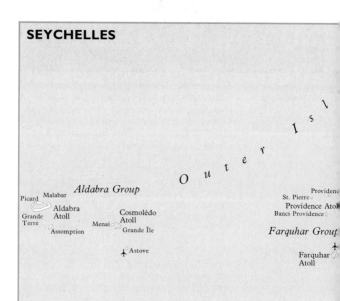

SEYCHELLES

Outer Islands

Aldabra Group

Picard Malabar
Grande Aldabra
Terre Atoll
  Assomption
Menai
Cosmolédo
Atoll
Grande Île
Astove

Providence
St. Pierre
Providence Atoll
Bancs Providence

Farquhar Group

Farquhar
Atoll

BACKGROUND

The islands and islets of the Seychelles archipelago are scattered over 154,000 square miles (400,000sq km) of the Indian Ocean between latitudes 4° and 11° south and longitudes 46° and 56° east. This makes

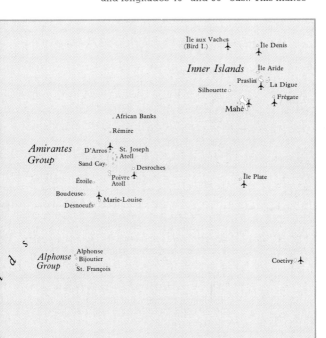

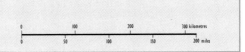

good sense to a yachtsman navigating the reefs, but arriving by air, you have the impression of landing on the edge of nowhere. Mahé, with the seat of government in Victoria, lies 980 miles (1,580km) east of Mombasa in Kenya and 1,750 miles (2,800km) southwest of Bombay. The distance between Mahé and the great southern atoll of Aldabra is 650 miles (1,045km), yet the entire land area of Seychelles covers only 175 square miles (453sq km).

The Islands

A complete inventory of all the islands is impossible. The generally accepted number is more or less 115, depending when this or that rock or reef is covered by the tide. Geologists categorise the islands into two types: granitic and coralline.

Seychelles, with the other Indian Ocean islands of Madagascar and Mauritius, is a vestige of the Precambrian mega-continent of Gondwanaland, which included all of present-day Africa, India and Australasia. Around 130 million years ago, this landmass broke up and the Indian Ocean flooded the great rifts, leaving only the mountain peaks above water. The 41 granitic Seychelles islands are effectively peaks of Gondwanaland. The 74 low, coralline islands are, by comparison, relatively recent formations, made from the skeletons of coral polyps and other marine animals. They include many atolls – ring-shaped reefs enclosing a lagoon. That of Aldabra was formed by the collapse of the central landmass.

The Inner Islands

The main islands in this, granitic, group are Mahé, Praslin, Silhouette and La Digue. Their highest point, Morne Seychellois in central Mahé, is at 2,970 feet (905m).

The islands are characterised by granite cliffs and rocky bays with a narrow coastal plain, often indented by lagoons. Hundreds of streams splash down to the sea from the central hills. In many places, extraordinary granite rocks stand in the bays like blobs of grey plasticine. Some are the size of houses, either worn smooth or wrinkled by millennia of erosion.

Coral Islands and Atolls

At the northern extremity of the archipelago are the flat, sandy islands of Denis and Bird (also called Île aux Vaches). Although part of the Inner Islands group, they are coralline and characterised by dazzling white beaches and coconut palms. Their maximum height above sea-level is under 16 feet (5m).

The rest of the archipelago, southwest of Mahé, consists entirely of coral islands, atolls

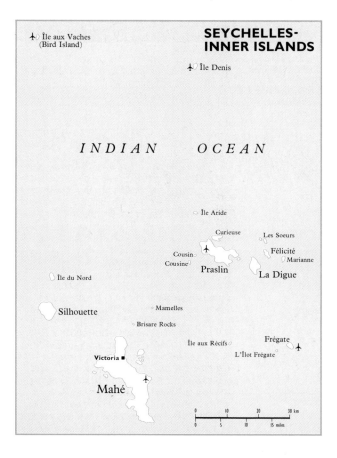

Île aux Vaches
(Bird Island)

**SEYCHELLES-
INNER ISLANDS**

Île Denis

INDIAN   OCEAN

Île Aride

Curieuse   Les Soeurs

Cousin   Félicité
Cousine   Marianne
Praslin   La Digue

Île du Nord

Mamelles

Silhouette

Brisare Rocks

Frégate
Île aux Récifs
L'Îlot Frégate

Victoria

Mahé

| 0 | 10 | 20 | 30 km |
| 0 | 5 | 10 | 15 miles |

BACKGROUND

Tropical sunset seen from the island of Denis, one of Seychelles' most peaceful resorts

and reefs. Except for Desroches, the nearest to Mahé, they are difficult to reach and have no facilities for visitors.

The group nearest to the Inner Islands, the **Amirantes**, is in line for development and includes Desroches – the only one of the group with an air link – Poivre, Desnoeufs, Saint Joseph Atoll and Marie-Louise. The tiny Alphonse group is just to the south.

The Outer Islands are classic castaway isles – flat and sandy with protective coral reefs. Guano, copra and fishing are the sole sources of income of their few inhabitants, for whom a visit to Mahé is exciting as a trip to the moon.

The **Farquar Group** includes the large atoll of Farquar with St Pierre and the rich fishing groups of the Bancs Providence.

West is the **Aldabra Group** which includes Cosmolédo, Assomption, Astove and the world's largest atoll, Aldabra. An airport is open on Assomption, but at the time of writing the region is not open to tourists and casual visitors.

A scientific reserve administered by the Seychelles Islands Foundation, Aldabra Atoll is 250 miles (400km) from the nearest mainland, Madagascar. Largely fossilised limestone, it has little soil, practically no fresh water and no deep-water anchorage. A supply vessel calls in only once every three months. The immense lagoon is large enough to swallow the entire island of Mahé. The tidal currents reach a speed of eight to twelve knots, flushing in and out schools of fish, sharks and rays.

Inhospitable, even dangerous... therein lies its protection not only from tourism, but even the minimum of human interference (only scientists go there). The colony of 150,000 giant tortoises, the flightless birds, the insects, the plants, the fabulous coral reefs and fish survive as part of a unique ecological system. See also **Peace and Quiet**.

History

It is only since the 18th century that human beings have inhabited the Seychelles. Arab sailors were probably the first to sight the islands during exploratory voyages off East Africa in the 9th century. The Portuguese explorer Vasco da Gama sighted an island at 4° south which he called 'Almirante', when he crossed the Indian Ocean at the end of the 15th century in an epoch-making journey. A Portuguese chart of about 1512 shows the Seychelles islands.

The first known British encounter with the islands was recorded in 1609 in the log of the *Ascension*, under the command of Captain Alexander Sharpeigh of the British East India Company. It describes rocky islands and sandy coves, coconuts, crocodiles and an abundance of 'tortells' ('turtles'), but again no mention of human life.

The First Settlements

The lack of interest in the Seychelles on the part of colonial sea-powers made it an ideal pirates' hideout. Chased from Caribbean waters, the most daring among them – the Britishers 'Long John' Avery, Captain Kidd and the notorious Frenchman Olivier le Vasseur ('La Buse') began harassing Indian Ocean shipping.

Faced with huge losses, British and French naval patrols managed to clear the area of pirates by the mid-18th century, but when Britain sought to add Seychelles to her eastern dominions, she found the French flag fluttering over Mahé.

The French had taken possession of the archipelago on 1 November 1756, when

BACKGROUND

Captain Nicolas Morphey had placed the 'Stone of Possession' on Mahé. Quietly colonised on behalf of the French king, the islands had been named after Louis XV's chancellor, Viscount Jean Moreau de Séchelles.

A first settlement was made on the east coast of Mahé (now the Mont Fleuri district) in 1770. The new community was a slow starter, but when African slaves were brought in to do the hard work, the forests began to be cleared for plantation farming. The islands' administrator (1767-72), appropriately named Pierre Poivre ('Peter Pepper'), encouraged spice-growing, especially pepper, cloves, chillis and cinnamon, imported from the East Indies.

Poivre was succeeded by Jean Baptiste Philogène de Malavois, an early conservationist, who deplored the damage being done by the settlers. In 1788, he banned felling of trees for firewood and the slaughter of all hawksbill turtles and tortoises (the giant tortoises had been almost exterminated). He declared a 'green zone' on Mahé, where no construction was allowed, a worthy law, only recently flouted by hotel-builders.

The 'treasure site' at Bel Ombre, Mahé, a vivid reminder that Seychelles was a haunt of pirates (see pages 32-4)

The British Takeover

Towards the end of the 18th century, attacks on British ships by French pirates, who were good customers for the produce of the Seychelles, led to conflict with France in the Indian Ocean.

As Britain increased her sea-patrols, France's hold on the isolated colony looked tenuous. Despite bitter rivalry in India, however, confrontation over Seychelles was largely non-violent until 1801, when a clash off Mahé left 35 French sailors dead.

Scenting victory, Britain dispatched a task force to demand that the French capitulate. The administrator of Seychelles, Jean-Baptiste Queau de Quinssy obeyed. The tricolour was brought down and the Union Jack run up the mast, but as soon as the British sailed away, the French standard was hoisted again. Communications being what they were at the time, the British had no idea the Frenchman was making fools of them. The farce was repeated seven times until the Seychelles, along with Île de France (or Mauritius) was officially ceded to Britain by the terms of the Treaty of Paris in 1814, making the Seychelles a dependency of Mauritius.

Liking the quirky Frenchman, the British invited de Quinssy to become the first governor of Seychelles. In accepting the position he had already held for 20 years, de Quinssy changed the spelling of his surname to the more Anglicised 'de Quincy'.

On his death in 1827, a street bearing both spellings, was named in his honour.

In 1827, Seychelles had 6,700 slaves compared to only 471 white colonists. The British abolished slavery in 1835, and this radically altered things. Slave labour had meant an easy lifestyle, farming profitable crops such as cotton, coffee, sugar cane and cloves. Now, unable to afford to pay the free workers a wage, the colonists allowed tracts of land to return to jungle. Less labour-intensive crops such as coconuts and vanilla became more important.

The arrival of thousands of liberated slaves and families from Mauritius saw the development of a new social order of fishermen and small farmers; Indians and Chinese immigrants took over trading and commerce.

On 31 August 1903, Seychelles was given the status of a British Crown Colony. By World War I, it had acquired the machinery of bureaucracy – a local currency, a postal service and the inevitable clock-tower, still standing in Victoria, the Seychelles' capital, albeit not always working – such as is found in former British colonies all over the world. Throughout their administration, the British found the Seychelles, isolated as they are, admirably suitable for exiling political opponents from their colonial possessions. Among various distinguished political prisoners exiled to Seychelles from British colonies were King Prempeh of Ashanti who arrived in 1900 with a retinue of 55 family-members and subjects; Mahmood Ali Shirreh, Sultan of the Warsangli tribe from the British Protectorate of Somaliland; Said Khalid bin Bargash, Pretender to the Sultanate of Zanzibar; and Archbishop Makarios of Cyprus.

One of the most colourful deportees was the former Sultan of Perak (in Malaya), Raja Abdullah Khan and his four wives and children who arrived in 1876. The sultan found Seychelles so enchanting that he took home a local song. Rehashed, it became the national anthem of independent Malaysia.

Republic of Seychelles

In 1948, a Legislative Council, with members elected by a limited franchise, was introduced, and political parties soon began to emerge. In 1970, Seychelles was given its first constitution, with universal adult franchise and an elected governing council. Elections that year brought to power the centre-right Seychelles Democratic Party (SDP), led by James Mancham, and the SDP increased its majority in elections in 1974. The Republic of Seychelles was declared under a coalition government on 29 June 1976. The coalition consisted of the SDP under Mancham (as president), and the socialist Seychelles People's United Party (later renamed the

The Sultan of Perak, one of the political exiles who enjoyed their exile in Seychelles as opponents of the British Empire

Seychelles People's Progressive Front), under Albert René (as prime minister). Mancham was ousted in a bloodless coup in 1977 after his flamboyant lifestyle displeased a radical socialist élite led by Albert René, who became president. One-party general elections were held in 1979, and a Seychellois-style of socialism was incorporated in a new constitution. As a result, many of the 'Grand Blanc' families (the original white settlers) emigrated to Britain, Canada, South Africa and Australia, where some established resistance movements. René survived several coup attempts, including a notorious one in 1981, when mercenaries pretending to be members of a South African rugby team, were discovered at the airport and routed. Since 1981, apart from a 48-hour military mutiny in 1982 (quickly suppressed), Seychelles has been peaceful and stable. In 1989, René was re-elected for a third (and, according to the constitution, last) term as president.

Seychelles Today
First time visitors to Seychelles may not be aware of the considerable achievements of the small island republic.

BACKGROUND

Economy

The most significant change in the last two decades is the development of a tourist industry. When the international airport opened on Mahé in 1971, only 5,000 visitors came that year. In a few years numbers will reach the annual limit, 140,000, set by the government to ensure the islands do not become overcrowded, with all the dangers to the environment which that entails.

Most visitors to Seychelles, up to 1990, came from Europe, but the government is campaigning to attract visitors from other parts of the world.

Tourism development has been carefully planned, with most hotels set back from the beach and only low-rise building (no higher than a coconut palm) permitted.

Almost all sectors of the local economy relate in some way to tourism. Practically everyone is, or has a relative, employed either directly in the hotel and catering trades, or in one of the ancillary industries such as watersports and crafts. While it is risky to rely on the fragile tourist industry – arrivals fell dramatically following news reports of the attempted coup in 1981 – Seychelles has few other options.

Bringing in the catch on Mahé: Traditional methods are being superseded by the technology of an up-to-date fishing industry

Manufacturing enterprises include soap, detergent, cigarettes, paint and biscuits, the packaging of tea and coffee, ceramics and diverse wooden crafts. Seychelles brews its own beer – and over one, or two, 'Seybrews',

talk turns to oil prospects. The government believes the chances of striking oil are positive, but in the short run, only fishing offers a real alternative economic base to tourism.

Fishermen have traditionally used basket-traps, nets and hand-lines. Hand-lining remains important, but radar and other sonic equipment have been introduced, and laws passed protecting local fisheries. Only Seychelles-owned and -registered fishing boats can now fish over the Seychelles plateau and five miles (8km) beyond its edge, although agreements with a number of countries regarding tuna fishing are still honoured. Important commercial exports include marlin, mackerel, bonito, snapper and barracuda – the value of canned tuna exports outstrips traditional earnings from copra and cinnamon bark. More than 300 permanent staff are employed by the tuna cannery, part of a large tuna fishery complex at Victoria harbour.

Seychelles is striving for self-sufficiency in agriculture, already achieved in poultry farming. It also produces 40 per cent of its beef requirements. The biggest farms are on Silhouette, Praslin and La Digue. Tea and coffee are grown on the western slopes of the Morne Seychellois mountains on Mahé.

Society and Religion

History has dictated the polyglot nature of Seychelles, whose population of around 70,000 lives mainly on Mahé. There are three official languages: English, French and Creole. The last was made official only recently, although 95 per cent of the population speak it as their first language. Creole is a patois of (archaic) French with African and English words incorporated. (See **Language** page 125.)

The modern Seychellois might have characteristics inherited from an original French settler, an African slave, a British colonist and an Asian immigrant.

It would be hard to find a greater melting-pot than Seychelles. It is an old joke that you don't ask whether a newborn infant is a boy, or a girl, but whether it is black, or white. Racism is unknown.

Today 90 per cent of Seychellois adhere to the Roman Catholic faith – there is a Catholic church, or at least a chapel, in every important community in Seychelles. (Anglicanism is marginal, although it can lay claim to one of Victoria's two cathedrals.) Archive records include a letter written to the governor of Seychelles, in 1851, by a member of the Savy family, still numerous locally, requesting the appointment of a priest and with a postscript saying he had made the request every year for the past 17 years. The first Roman Catholic clergy arrived in 1853 causing alarm among the extant Protestant church, as Catholicism soon caught on with the majority. (For more information on Seychellois life, see **How to be a Local** page 102.)

Government

The Republic of Seychelles is a one-party state, that party being President René's Seychelles People's Progressive Front. Opposition to the ruling party is not overt. The president, who is head of both state and government, holds executive power and is directly elected for a five-year term. The National Assembly consists of one chamber with 23 elected and two appointed members. A series of five-year plans, announced in 1979, improved local living standards. Policies include free education and medical treatment, and increased public housing.

Conservation

The Seychelles government has a positive attitude towards conservation. As well as controlling development projects, it has designated a number of areas of particular environmental importance as national parks and reserves.

The waters of Seychelles are a protected area for whales, which may not be hunted here for any reason. In addition, the government has proposed to the International Whaling Commission the establishment of an Indian Ocean sanctuary for all marine mammals.

MAHÉ

Mahé is the biggest island, the administrative and commercial centre and the tourist hub of Seychelles. Yet it is unspoilt. The turquoise ocean washing magical beaches is quintessential Seychelles. Among the most beautiful islands in the world, Mahé offers beaches, watersports and nature trails on the one hand, and the colourful town life of Victoria, the capital, on the other. Seychelles International Airport is on the east coast, 20 minutes' drive from Victoria. The new highway is the only straight road on the island; others wind over the mountains and curl round the coast, which is indented by 68 bays. Mahé is only 17 miles (27km) long and five miles (8km) across, but it is normal for a rented vehicle to register as much as 50,000km when you take it over.

The emerald coastline is characterised by great granite outcrops. Baie Lazare, on southwest Mahé, was the site of the first planned landing in the Seychelles archipelago on 10 August 1742. Captain Lazare Picault spent three months exploring the inner granitic islands. He gave his name to the bay where he landed. That of his employer, Bertrand François Mahé, comte de La Bourdonnais, (governor of Mauritius) was given to the whole island. Returning to Île de France, as Mauritius was once known, the MV *Elisabeth* carried a cargo of coconuts and 300 giant land tortoises. Slaves brought to the island by the first settlers after 1770 cleared much of Mahé's native vegetation to cultivate copra, spices and tea. People still live in the narrow coastal zone with their backs to the mountains

Street scene in Victoria

MAHÉ

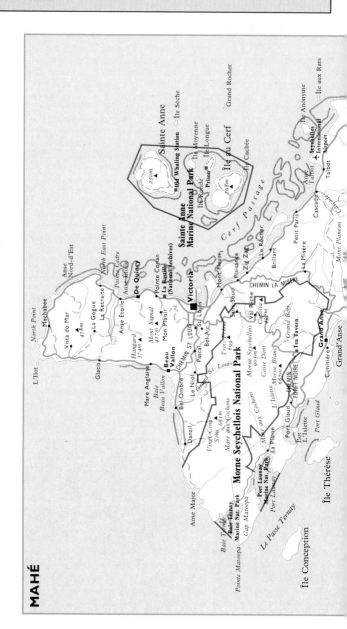

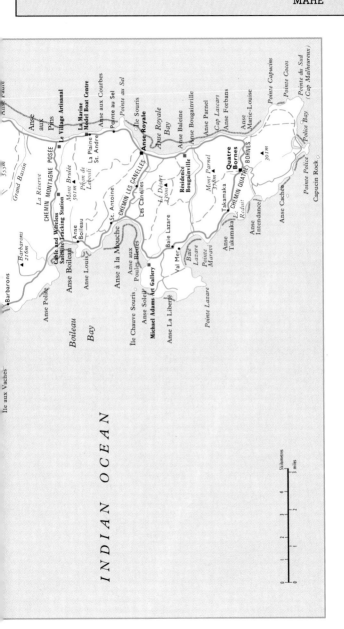

and their eyes on the sea. Settlement has recently pushed up the mountainsides around Victoria, but there are valleys in mountainous central Mahé never explored by man. Southern Mahé is also wild and undeveloped.

Mahé, like the other islands, experiences two wind seasons a year. When the boisterous southeast trades blow from May to October, the west coast which includes the Beau Vallon area is protected, while Victoria and the east coast lie in the lee of the northwest monsoon from November to April.

The weather on Mahé varies greatly in a day, but with transport and a 'weather-eye', you can usually find a calm, sunny bay.

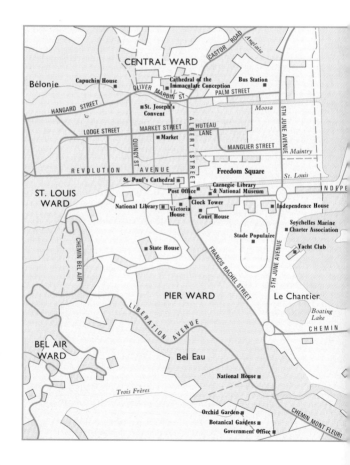

VICTORIA

Victoria is the pocket-sized, capital of Seychelles, at the foot of Morne Seychellois. Around 40,000 people live in the town and its environs of Saint Louis, Mont Fleuri and Bel Air.

In the centre of town is a miniature version of Big Ben in London. Painted silver, it stands on the junction of Albert Street and Independence Avenue. Until recently, the clock struck twice – once on the hour and again two minutes later. Some said it was for those hard of hearing; others said it was to remind the laid-back Seychellois that time was passing.

Although small and unpretentious, Victoria puts more sophisticated cities to shame. No one would dream of dropping litter and the streets are swept clean.

By dusk most workers have drifted home. Government offices close at 17.00 hrs when the exodus is considerable. By the time the cathedral bell tolls at 19.00 hrs you can hear birds twittering in the trees.

Tourism did not really exist prior to the opening of the airport in 1971. Early visitors to Seychelles on the long voyage from Mombasa and other Indian Ocean ports might notice a few changes. Victoria counts around a dozen more buildings, mainly banks, travel agents and boutiques. There is a new port, a national stadium and a winged statue on Freedom Square, whose meaning is unclear; some say it represents the continents of Europe, Africa and Asia.

Architecture

Coming from Europe, or America, you are more likely to be impressed by Victoria's old-style architecture. A marriage of colonial and 'Indian Ocean style' it is pure Seychellois. Sadly many of the old residences have been

VICTORIA

ong Pier
ENCE   AVENUE

**Interisland
Ferry Terminal**

Île Hodoul

*Inner
Harbour*

New Port

ATANIER

VELOUTIER ROAD

0   100   200   300   400 metres

demolished. Other buildings have been modified, or fallen into disrepair.

Hard-wood tile roofs have suffered greatly in the hot, wet climate. Today most houses display corrugated iron roofs. Many are designed so that they are a feature, rather than just a lid. Painted different colours, they have faded into attractive pastel shades. **Marie-Antoinette Restaurant** is in one of the most striking old houses in Victoria. The explorer Stanley rested here after his exhausting search and meeting in Africa with Dr Livingstone, when it was known as the 'Grand Trianon'.

Victoria's Botanical Gardens

WHAT TO SEE IN VICTORIA
♦♦♦
BOTANICAL GARDENS
off Chemin Mont Fleuri

The Botanical Gardens at the foot of Mont Fleuri, are 10 minutes' walk from Victoria. The turn before the Mont Fleuri Hospital is well indicated. The beautifully landscaped gardens cover 15 acres (6 hectares). They were created in 1901 by a Frenchman, Rivaltz Dupont. Among six endemic species of Seychelles palms in the gardens is the famous coco-de-mer (see page 88). If you are not going to visit the Vallée de Mai on Praslin, where the coco-de-mer grows wild, this is an opportunity to see it growing. Walking up the main driveway you pass several young coco-de-mer palms and the strange bottle palms from Mauritius. Among many striking plants in the gardens are the handsome vacoa parasol screwpine, the lobster claw from South America, the torch ginger plant known for its striking pink flowers, and the spreading traveller's palms – both the latter from Madagascar. In the orchid garden, note the giant orchid from Java. Its ten-foot (3m) long stems are ever flowering. The cannon ball tree whose nuts grow straight out of the trunk is another exotic plant. There is also a replica of a wetland on La Digue.

Allow yourself two hours. A cafeteria sells refreshments and there is a WC.

Open: daily 08.00-18.00hrs. Admission free.

♦♦♦
COLONIAL BUILDINGS

The old **Court House and Treasury** near the clock-tower is one of Victoria's most elegant colonial-style buildings. The small fountain in the grounds opposite the Post Office was originally graced with a statue of Queen Victoria, (now in the National Museum). Around the Albert Street side is a bust of Pierre Poivre (see page 12).

The **National Library** is another fine building surrounded by a wrought iron balcony. Continuing down the same road, **State House** at the end is another grand old mansion. It now houses the presidential offices.

The biggest edifice in Victoria is the **Archbishopric** which occupies a block on Olivier Mardin Street. It is near **Saint**

The huge Archbishopric dwarfs most of Victoria's other buildings

Joseph's Convent and the **Cathedral of the Immaculate Conception**. You will come across other old architectural gems when you least expect to.

♦
HARBOUR

The harbour is functional rather than attractive. The best views are obtained from the sea on a boat-trip to Sainte Anne Marine National Park. **Marine Charter** on 5th June Avenue is the departure-point for marine excursions and fishing trips. The **Yacht Club** is open to non-members seeking contacts. Interisland shipping departs from the **Interisland Ferry Terminal** (see map page 22–23).

◆◆◆
MARKET
Market Street

Formerly called Sir Selwyn Selwyn Clarke Market – the sign is still on the gate – Victoria's open market, or bazaar, sells everything from sharks' jaws to cinnamon sticks and a variety of souvenirs. The best day is Saturday, when all Mahé rubs shoulders around the stalls. The fish market is especially busy as vendors chop up huge mackerel, bonito and kingfish. The buyer carries off the lump of fish swinging on a length of string. Nothing is wasted – you often see people carrying only a fish-head to make fish soup. The market is a kaleidoscope of free-wheeling local enterprise: fish on the left of the gate on Market Street, crafts and fruit in the centre and vegetables arranged under the spreading tree. Lettuce and other salads are dunked in a pond, shaken free of water and stuffed in a customer's bag. White egrets or 'Madame Patons' strut ceremoniously about after scraps.

Local fruits and vegetables on display in Victoria's busy market

◆◆◆
NATIONAL ARCHIVES

*La Bastille, about a mile (2km)
north of Victoria*
You can find La Bastille, an old
house which contains the
National Archives, by taking a
left turn past Pointe Conan.
Parking is available. Ask to
see the First Issue and
Independence Day stamps,
and the poignant lists of
African slaves. Staff are
helpful.
Open: Monday to Friday
08.00-16.00hrs, Saturday
08.00-12.00hrs.
Admission free.

*List of freed African slaves in the
National Archives*

◆◆◆
NATIONAL MUSEUM

Independence Avenue
Situated next to the Post Office,
the museum at first seems
bland. A closer look reveals a
treasure-trove of artefacts.
The Stone of Possession, laid to
mark French possession of
Seychelles in 1756, is opposite
the entrance. The stone bears
the Fleur-de-lis of France and
the crown of Louis XV and is
Seychelles' oldest relic.
In the left front room is a copy
of the proclamation of the
Capitulation of Seychelles as
heard by Captain Henry
Newcome of HM *Orpheus*. It
reads:
'...I give you one hour from the
delivery of this message to
decide. If any resistance is
made, you must abide by the
consequences thereof, 16th
May 1794.'
Another interesting document
in this room is the list of
original French settlers and a
tally of Ashanti prisoners who
accompanied King Edward
Prempeh into exile in 1900.
There is an eclectic
assemblage of objects, which
includes turtle-shell
snuffboxes, tin coffee
percolators and coconut
utensils. Pirate memorabilia is
also on display. A stone model
of a pirate's tombstone is
inscribed with a skull-and-
crossbones and these words:
*Jean-Pierre Le Chartier, Tué le
4 mars 1805 par son ami
Evellon. Passants priez pour
moi* – 'Jean-Pierre Le Chartier,
killed on 4 March 1805 by his
friend Evellon. Passers-by,
pray for me.'
The small ceramic statue of
Queen Victoria holding the
globe, which once adorned the
fountain opposite the post
office in Victoria is now housed
in the National Museum.
Open: weekdays
09.00-17.00hrs, Saturday
09.00-12.00hrs. Admission free.

AROUND THE COAST

Most people will start a round trip of the island from Victoria. From the clock-tower, drive down Independence Avenue and turn right at the roundabout. You will have the harbour on your left and the national stadium to your right. At the second roundabout, take the Chemin Mont Fleuri to go down the east coast. A new airport road, starting from the same roundabout and built on reclaimed land will, when completed, provide a faster journey and good views on the way.

South from Victoria

By the time you reach the small settlement of **Cascade**, you will feel 'in the country'. The local Church of Saint André has some fine stained-glass windows and there is a good view. Beyond here the road winds past the Reef Hotel and Mahé golf-course. At Pointe au Sel, you have a view of **Anse Royale**. The coastal road next passes **La Résidence Bougainville**, a fine old colonial-style guesthouse which is worth a stop (see page 46). Park at the top of the steep drive.

South of here, the road veers inland for Quatre Bornes village *en route* to Takamaka on the southwest coast. A track (Chemin Grande Police) leads from Quatre Bornes to **Anse Intendance and Police Bay**. It is a beautiful drive from Takamaka to **Baie Lazare** via Pointe Maravi where the **Lazare Picault** guesthouse (see page 42) has a stunning site.

The smallest shop in Victoria

◆◆◆
OLD VICTORIA

Explore Victoria on foot as its one-way streets are confusing by car. The area is too small for you to get lost.

Many old 'Indian Ocean style' shops are seen around Market Street, Church Street and Huteau Lane. Quincy Street/Rue de Quinssy is named after the first governor of British Seychelles. Colourful general stores line Francis Rachel street. Most are Indian owned. The smallest, a tailor's, is little bigger than a couple of telephone booths. Yellow, red and green are popular colours. The brown-red of rust is everywhere.

There are several restaurants around here, or you can stop at the **Plantation Club**. The road cuts inland here, reaching the coast again at **Anse aux Poules Bleues**. **Michael Adams Art Gallery** here is an essential stop (see page 98).

The West Coast

The road up the west coast of Mahé follows the shoreline around **Anse à la Mouche**, **Anse Boileau** and **Grand'Anse** to Port Glaud. You can proceed no further north here as it is a prohibited area beyond.

The scenery all along the west coast is very lush, and beyond the Barbarons Estate to the north of Anse Boileau are vast coconut plantations. Travelling north up the coast you pass a big tropical nursery and orchid farm – near the Meridien Barbarons Hotel – open 09.00–19.00hrs weekdays (closed weekends). There are mangrove swamps in this area and near Port Glaud (see **Peace and Quiet**, page 85). When you reach the Sheraton at Port Glaud, you have covered two-thirds of Mahé. A visit to offshore **L'lslette** is recommended from here (see page 38).

The North

By now, you probably realise that Mahé is bigger than it seems. It is a bold visitor who drives round the island in a single day. You require two to three days to take in the attractions (see **What to See** below), and four to five days to include swimming and leisurely lunches. The largest concentration of hotels on Mahé is at **Beau Vallon** on the northwest coast. It is not possible to drive here directly from Port Glaud (see above). You must return to Victoria by the Chemin Forêt Noire (see page 36) and then take the Chemin St Louis. The coastal road continues north from Beau Vallon.

North Point is an exposed area opposite North Island, where young people do their two years' compulsory national service. On this stretch of coast at Northeast Point, you will find **Kreolfleurage**, an unusual perfumery (see page 34).

In the Michael Adams Art Gallery at Anse aux Poules Bleues, Mahé

Northeast Mahé is drier and more built up than the lush west coast, and has little to offer, but you have to include it on the circle island road. The tiny settlement of De Quincy enjoys good views of Sainte Anne Marine National Park (see page 39). From here you are soon back in Victoria.

WHAT TO SEE
(including beaches)

Mahé is reckoned to have 68 beaches. The most popular beaches or *anses* – the French word for a small bay – are included below. Those mentioned are all seen on a circle-island tour but you may find more of your own. The more secluded the beach, the more careful you should be swimming: currents can sweep you out to sea ... and it is *not* ghost-crabs that take belongings left on the beach.

◆◆
ANSE À LA MOUCHE

This calm, palm-lined bay is on the southwest coast. It is good for swimming and snorkelling, and has several restaurants. To get there from the east coast take the short mountain road over Les Cannelles.

◆◆◆
ANSE AUX PINS

This is a long beach south from the Reef Hotel on the east coast. Palms extending over the lagoon make it a perfect photo-location. The beach tends to be inundated at high-tide, but offers good swimming and snorkelling. Windsurfing is popular near the Reef Hotel. Facilities include a general store, bank and several restaurants. It is exposed to the southeast trade winds.

Anse aux Pins, Mahé

Tiny Île Souris off Anse Royale

◆◆
ANSE INTENDANCE AND POLICE BAY

Two long, sandy beaches at the southern tip of Mahé, they are fringed by tall coconut-palms including a rare, double-coconut. They are ideal if you want to get away from the crowd at Beau Vallon. Take snacks and drinks as there are no shops. Watch your things. There may be a considerable surf from May to September.

◆
ANSE MARIE-LOUISE AND ANSE FORBANS

These are attractive southeast beaches, not visible from the road and quiet – the only other people you are likely to see are fishermen. Nearest facilities are at La Résidence Bougainville to the north (see page 46).

◆◆◆
ANSE ROYALE

This is one of the biggest bays in Seychelles. It is the main east coast beach with numerous sandy inlets. The offshore coral reef protects the lagoon with the best snorkelling on Mahé. There is also excellent fishing; a good place to watch fishermen coming and going.

A secluded bay near Île Souris is known as 'Lover's Beach'. You need to watch your gear here.

The village has a store, petrol station and restaurant – **Kaz Creole** (delightful lunch-stop if you are not on a budget – see **Restaurants** page 48). On the south side is a traditional Seychellois house although its rose garden is unusual in the tropics.

Watersports at Beau Vallon Bay

◆◆◆
ANSE TAKAMAKA

A lovely beach to the south of Baie Lazare, with a good, Creole-style restaurant. Typical scenery of waving palms and glistening granite rocks. Locals flock here at weekends. It may be rough during the southeast trades. Beware of currents.

◆◆
BAIE LAZARE

On the southwest coast, this is where the first landing was made in 1742. Either end is flanked by sentinels of granite. Beware of dangerous currents at Val Mer. There are shady trees and it is the location of the Plantation Club hotel.

◆◆◆
BEAU VALLON BAY (BAIE BEAU VALLON)

The bay is in the northwest only 12 minutes' drive from Victoria. Shaded by *takamaka* trees and coconut palms, this is the best known beach in Seychelles, with 2½ miles (4km) of sand, excellent swimming and the main watersports centre on Mahé. It has a dive-shop, beach bars, hotels and restaurants. Calm May-October.

◆◆◆
BEL OMBRE

A small beach at the southern end of Beau Vallon Bay, this is a place with a fascinating story of pirate treasure.
Tales of buried treasure are legion in Seychelles, as Mahé

in particular was a popular base for pirate attacks on shipping.

The last of the old-style treasure-hunters was an Englishman, Reginald Cruise-Wilkins, who died in 1977 after spending 30 years looking for the treasure hidden by the French pirate, Olivier le Vasseur, known as 'La Buse' (the Buzzard).

His biggest prize was *La Vierge du Cap*, a Portuguese vessel captured around 1720 on a voyage from Goa to Lisbon. Its cargo included £100 million in gold and silver sovereigns, 18 boxes of diamonds, the Portuguese Viceroy's jewellery and a ruby-studded cross from the Bom Jesus Cathedral known as the 'Fiery Cross of Goa'.

As 'La Buse' was about to be hanged in Réunion in 1730, he is said to have flung a batch of documents at the crowd with the cry: 'Find my treasure who can!'.

Cruise-Wilkins, a former game-warden in Kenya, believed La Buse hid the treasure on Mahé, at Bel Ombre. An early map of Mahé had the words 'Owner of land –La Buse' written over the area at the southern end of Beau Vallon Bay.

Cruise-Wilkins obtained a cryptic parchment diagram found in the National Archives in Mauritius, another pirate haunt. When he heard that skeletons with gold earrings had been dug up, Cruise-Wilkins set out to crack the cryptogram.

Odd clues convinced him that

La Buse – a known student of Greek and Latin – had based his clues on Greek mythology: the word 'Jason' in the cryptogram he took to mean Jason and the Argonauts and their search for the Golden Fleece.

At first Cruise-Wilkins found nothing because La Buse had used 18th-century measurements. Metric recalculations led him to the beach at Bel Ombre, where his men dug up the skeleton of a horse. But it was no ordinary horse: its forelegs were broken and pushed through the rib-cage to resemble wings. He took this as another clue from Greek mythology: Pegasus, the winged horse.

Continuing the theme of Greek mythology, Cruise concluded that 'La Buse' must have laid the clues to represent the 12 Labours of Hercules. Hercules was the Greek hero – later worshipped as a god – who, in order to achieve immortality, had to complete 12 stupendous labours, such as cleaning the Augean stables where 300 oxen had lived for 30 years and finding the golden apples of the Hesperides.

Each clue discovered on the 60-acre (25-hectare) site matched the cryptogram. A pig's jaw-bone found near tide level, the treasure-hunters took to mean they were nearing the treasure: Hercules had to slay a sow before descending into the Underworld. On an enormous granite rock, Cruise found an engraving of Cerberus, the three-headed canine guardian of Hell. The rusty water around the base of the rock, Cruise declared, came from bindings on the treasure chests.

But he never managed the 12th labour. Broke, he had raised £43,000 by selling treasure shares to loyal followers. This too had gone and his labourers left. Workers constructing Mahé's new airport were unwilling to help with their bulldozers, and to this day the treasure has never been located. You will see a flag, with a skull and cross-bones, fluttering over the 'site' at Bel Ombre.

There is a hotel and restaurant at Bel Ombre beach.

From Sunset Beach Hotel, Glacis

◆◆◆ CARANA BEACH

To the north of Glacis is Carana Beach – a perfect spot for pirates to hide their treasure. Park and climb over the granite rocks to reach good swimming. It is protected from wind June to September. There are no facilities.

◆◆◆ GLACIS

Glacis, north of Beau Vallon, enjoys some of the most beautiful scenery in Seychelles. Houses at the end of concealed driveways look through palm-trees towards the turquoise sea.

◆ GRAND'ANSE

The bay is on the west coast between the hotels Equator and Meridien Barbarons. The long, white beach is lined with *takamaka* trees. There is a lively surf, especially from November to April.

◆ KREOLFLEURAGE NATIVE PERFUMES

Kreolfleurage is the inspiration of a German micro-biologist, Pit Hugelmann, who settled here in 1978. Now naturalised, he has created three ethnic perfumes using 20 per cent native plants picked on Morne Seychellois, and around Police Bay. Some must be harvested at precisely the right time: the frangipani just before it falls, or the hibiscus just before it opens.

'Bwanwar', one of the exotic

La Marine Model Boat Centre

scents produced, is made of 42 different essences – among them vetiver, patchouli, vanilla, cinnamon bark and passionfruit flower.

◆◆◆
LA MARINE MODEL BOAT CENTRE
A blue sign indicates 'La Marine' at La Plaine Saint Andre, about five miles (8km) south of the airport. This is the last place in the Indian Ocean where model boats are made by hand. The 15 young Seychellois employed here make everything to scale from designs obtained from the French Naval Museum in Paris. Women make the rigging. About ten models are made a month.
Open: daily; until 16.00hrs on Saturday.

◆◆◆
LE VILLAGE ARTISANAL
Le Village Artisanal (Crafts Village) is at Anse aux Pins. You could probably pass an hour looking at the workshops and galleries – it is a good spot to shop for souvenirs. A house in the village centre has been furnished to depict early 'plantation lifestyle'. It contains some good furniture and other artefacts. You might like to have a Creole-lunch at **Pomme Canelle** restaurant.
Open: Monday to Friday 08.00-17.00hrs., Saturday 09.00-17.00hrs. Closed Sunday.

◆◆◆
SUNSET BEACH
Sunset Beach at Glacis is overlooked by the Sunset Hotel. This jewel-like cove with shady trees offers calm swimming, diving and fishing off the rocks.

MAHÉ

INLAND MAHÉ

A number of roads cross Mahé, linking the east and west coasts. They are of varying length and interest.

♦♦♦
CHEMIN FORÊT NOIRE
one hour's drive
This is by far the most interesting mountain road crossing Mahé. While not steep, it is extremely circuitous. The heights of Morne Seychellois are cool after the humid coast: you may need a sweater.
The initial road is the Chemin Sans Souci from Victoria to Val

Chemin Sans Souci, Mahé

Riche; it passes several old colonial homes. Many of the houses – missions and embassies – are concealed by forest. On the left of a sharp curve is the United States Embassy where Archbishop Makarios was incarcerated during his exile in Seychelles. The cascade is a good spot to park. Traffic is not heavy, so you may hear bird-song. Leave the car for a shady two-hour walk.

Val Riche-Copolia Nature Trail

This walk cuts through Morne Seychellois National Park (*No 8 Nature Trails and Walks in Seychelles*).

Although classed 'medium', the trail is steep, dipping into the valley and ascending to a huge slab of granite, or *glacis* 1,600 feet (500m) above sea-level. Watch out for pitcher plants and other unique flora on the higher sections of the trail. For further information on fauna and flora of Mahé see **Peace and Quiet**.

Tea Tavern

After crossing Morne Blanc (2,188 feet/667m), the Chemin Forêt Noire is lined with tea estates. A stop at the tea tavern is recommended for a cup of tea and a visit to the tea factory. A shop sells a variety of Indian Ocean teas including mint, lemon grass and vanilla. *Tavern and factory open*: Monday to Friday 08.00-17.00hrs.

It is ten minutes' downhill drive to the west coast. On a clear day there are views of Île Thérèse and the Sheraton Hotel at Port Glaud.

◆
CHEMIN LA MISÈRE
45 minutes' drive
This road goes from Grand' Anse on the west coast to the outskirts of Victoria, a winding, misty route across central Mahé. It passes the ruins of a mission founded in 1875 for the education of orphaned slave children.

◆
CHEMIN MONTAGNE POSÉE
35 minutes' drive
From Anse Boileau on the west to Anse aux Pins on the east, this is a cool, often misty road, passing the Cable and Wireless Satellite tracking station on La Réserve. A nature trail goes from here to Mont Brulée (1,643 feet/501m).

Other roads crossing Mahé are:
Chemin St Louis, linking Victoria and Beau Vallon. This is the most familiar cross-island route for most visitors, a busy road to be avoided at peak hours – 07.00-09.00hrs and 16.00-17.30hrs.
Chemin Les Canelles, a short cut across southern Mahé from Anse Royale to Anse La Mouche. Of no particular interest, this drive takes about 20 minutes.
Chemin Quatre Bornes, followed by anyone making the island circuit round the coast (see page 28). The route crosses Mahé about a mile and a half (2km) north of the island's southern extremity.

EXCURSIONS FROM MAHÉ

◆◆◆
L'ISLETTE

L'Islette is a tiny island as its name suggests. It lies about 220 yards (200m) off Port Glaud Bay on the west coast of Mahé. Hail the ferry-man who provides a free boat service – or if the tide is in you can swim across.

Most visitors to L'Islette come for the day only, but you can also stay. The island has four comfortable chalets. Families are accommodated in spacious rooms in part of the owner's house. There is also spectacular accommodation for newlyweds in a bungalow built on a secluded granite outcrop. Called 'Honeymoon on the Rocks', it overlooks Île Thérèse.

Guests staying on L'Islette take half-board. The only place to

L'Islette is a place for relaxation

Sainte Anne Marine National Park, a popular day-trip from Mahé

eat is in the palm-thatched restaurant-bar by the ferry-landing. The menu is big on seafood. The house speciality is *Spaghetti à L'Islette* – with prawns, smoked fish and octopus. At lunchtime on Sunday there is a Creole barbecue. Meals are moderately priced and the island is licensed.

Activities on L'Islette are swimming, snorkelling and fishing. You cannot walk far as it covers only seven acres (3 hectares). The nearest hotel is the Seychelles Sheraton, a one mile (1.5km) walk along the coast. Several mangrove swamps around Port Glaud may interest nature-lovers. The coast road terminates beyond the village which has a local-type restaurant and a shop.
L'Islette off Port Glaud, Mahé (tel: 78229). Moderate prices.

snorkelling stop on the reefs. There are good views of Mahé on the way out. The park is protected from the southeast trades and the sea is usually calm. A pamphlet explains various spots of interest in the marine park.

Some 150 species of fish have been identified on the local reefs. You can see many from the sub-aqua boat which has comfortable seating below water-line. The Travel Services Seychelles guide can identify most common varieties as well as the different corals. Off northwest Sainte Anne is a starker world of steep granite rocks and waving weed. Extensive grass beds between Île au Cerf and Ronde lure green turtles to feed at night. Good clumps of coral in the pass between Île au Cerf and Île Longue attract jewel-like fish. Visibility is normally around 16-26 feet (5-8m), but coral dust may restrict viewing during big tides.

Île au Cerf

The island is privately owned and has about 40-50 inhabitants. The **Beach Shed Bar-Restaurant** is open Tuesday, Friday and Sunday, but you must book in advance through the Marine Charter Association on Mahé. Cerf is a favourite weekend boat-trip with Mahé families. Fifteen minutes from Victoria, it is a well wooded island, one mile (1.7km) long and half a mile (900m) across. There is safe swimming in front of the restaurant and good snorkelling off the north coast.

♦♦♦
SAINTE ANNE MARINE NATIONAL PARK

Off the northeast coast, this is the most popular day-trip for tourists on Mahé. Established in 1973, it encloses five islands – Île au Cerf, Île Longue, Île Moyenne, Île Ronde, and Sainte Anne. Every living creature within its boundaries is protected.

Travel Services Seychelles and other Mahé tour operators organise day excursions to several islands in the marine park.

The boat-trip leaves Marine Charter on Victoria Harbour at 09.30 hrs. The cost includes hotel transfers, snorkelling, a glass-bottom boat trip and sub-aqua ride, and lunch on Île Moyenne or Ronde. There is time for swimming and exploring, with the return scheduled around 16.00hrs.

It takes about 20 minutes from Marine Charter to a

Île Longue

This is an island prison and may not be visited. At the time of writing, it held 140 inmates, mainly sentenced for drugs offences. Longue is among the islands seen on the approach to Seychelles International Airport on Mahé.

Île Moyenne

The island is open three times a week to excursion boats. It is owned by Brendon Grimshaw, a former journalist, raconteur and genial host. His side-kick is Derek, Moyenne's giant land tortoise who can shake hands like a trained spaniel. An uninhibited reptile, Derek's star act is to mate in public. Alfred d'Emmerez de Chamoy bought the island for 301 rupees in 1892. Grimshaw

Brendon Grimshaw, owner of Moyene island, with Derek and friend

purchased Moyenne 18 years ago. Like many local islomanes, he believes in buried pirate treasure. He also says the island is inhabited by ghosts.

Island Walk

The circumambulation record on Moyenne is 4 minutes and 28 seconds. Walking slowly, you can complete the circuit in 45 minutes on a trail that took Grimshaw seven years to hack out of the undergrowth. The less agile may find it steep in places, but children can manage without difficulty. Ordinary gym boots are suitable for the terrain.

The trail passes a ruined house where Miss Emma Wardlow Best, a one-time owner of the island, lived with her collection of stray dogs. Her will in 1919 had the proviso that nothing – not even a rat – was to be killed. The injunction still applies. Moyenne skinks (a type of lizard) are so bold they will come up and drink the perspiration droplets on your legs.

Not far from the restaurant (see below) is a small consecrated chapel and cemetery. Beyond here, in the scrub on your right, is a sign marked 'Julie's Favourite Haunt'. Julie and her husband, a carpenter, married as teenagers and lived on Moyenne for 42 years.

Facilities

The boat moors off 'I Don't Care Beach' on Moyenne's southern shore. It is an easy climb up to the hilltop restaurant-bar.

Everything has to be imported

from Mahé. The restaurant sells soft drinks and ice-cold beer. Its Creole buffet-style lunch includes fried aubergine, grilled fish, salads and curry.

A score of native trees have been planted. A budding coco-de-mer can be seen near the bar. Birds such as cardinals and turtle doves have been introduced from other islands. Moyenne now counts several hundred birds which consume two sacks of rice a month.

Île Ronde
Equidistant from Île Moyenne and Longue, Île Ronde swells like an emerald in an aquamarine setting. Close to, it resembles a floating forest, being perfectly round and bristling with vegetation. The sand-banks on the Sainte Anne side of the island are alive with crabs and sea birds.

Chez Gaby dishes up some of Seychelles' tastiest Creole food. Grilled tuna steaks are especially good. The island was once a leprosarium with a chapel, clinic and small prison for miscreants. Its cells have become Gaby's bar and kitchen.

Sainte Anne
The biggest offshore island in the marine park, Sainte Anne lies three miles (5km) off Mahé and rises to a height of 820 feet (250m). A southern coral reef offers good snorkelling. Boat-trips moor off here for skin-diving and sub-sea viewing. Sainte Anne is government owned and visitors may not land. There is an old whaling station on the south point.

Accommodation
Hotels
Auberge Club Des Seychelles, PO Box 526, Bel Ombre, Mahé, (tel: 47550). Owned by Paradise Resorts, with 40 rooms and in a quiet position at the end of Bel Ombre (4½ miles/7km from Victoria). Built on the headland with a swimming pool at sea-level. Babysitting by arrangement. Night-bar open: midnight-07.00hrs. Children 2-12 free accommodation during high/low season, provided they are sharing with two full paying adults. Moderate.

Beau-Vallon Bay Hotel, PO Box 550, Beau Vallon, Mahé (tel: 47414). 184-room block-style hotel on Beau Vallon Beach, 10 minutes' drive from Victoria. All rooms are air-conditioned with bath-shower. Swimming pool on the beach. New fully-equipped Watersports Centre for windsurfing, canoeing, sailing, diving with trained instructors. The best beach on Mahé for swimming. Ideal for families – baby-sitting by arrangement. Children's video-games room. Main restaurant provides excellent breakfast buffet, lunch and dinner. Beachside pizzeria-Chinese restaurant – bookings essential (19.00-23.00hrs). Entertainment includes poolside cabaret, nightly dancing and Casino (see page 48). Shops, mini-golf, floodlit tennis. Taxi-rank. Expensive.

Casuarina Beach Hotel, PO Box 338, Victoria, Mahé, (tel: 76211). A charming small hotel at Anse aux Pins, about 10 minutes' drive from Seychelles International Airport. 16 comfortable rooms under shady pines. Small, quiet beach. Sports facilities at the nearby Reef Hotel. Rustic, palm-thatch restaurant with Continental and Creole cooking (spoilt by surly service). Gets the wind during Christmas period, sheltered June-August. Children accepted, aged 2-11 at 50 per cent of adult rate. Moderate.

Coral Strand Hotel, PO Box 400, Mahé (tel: 47036). Situated on the beach near the Beau Vallon Bay Hotel. 102 rooms with air-conditioning and mini-bar. Well located for all watersports. Scuba-diving centre and shop. Popular beach bar and main beach-front restaurant. Entertainment includes barbecue-cabaret, dancing. Day-room also available 1-4 hours. Full wedding service with photographer, bridesmaid, flowers etc. Expensive.

Equator Grand'Anse Residence, PO Box 526, Grand'Anse, Mahé (tel: 78228). A member of the Paradise Resorts chain, this is an up-market package tour hotel on the west coast, removed from mainstream Mahé. 56 duplex-suites (suites on two levels), all with mini-bar, refrigerator and tea-making facilities. Some have lounge plus balcony. The main recreation area overlooks the sea. Swimming-pool. Tennis, billiards and watersports by arrangement. Regular evening entertainment. Good

atmosphere suited to young-middle aged tourists. Transport essential – about 40 minutes' drive from Victoria. Expensive.

Hotel Lazare Picault, PO Box 135, Victoria, Mahé (tel: 71117). 14 simple but comfortable rooms (including singles) for people wanting to escape the mainstream. In a spectacular position overlooking the Baie Lazare. Small, romantic bar-restaurant. Swimming, snorkelling and fishing in Baie Lazare. Transport essential. Unsuitable for children and elderly tourists because of its hillside position well away from the beach. Ideal for a self-contained, independent traveller. Moderate.

Le Meridien Barbarons, PO Box 626, Mahé (tel: 78253). 125 rooms along a white sand beach on the west coast of Mahé. Transport essential for sightseeing – 40 minutes from Victoria. Relaxed, but bland, with large swimming-pool, windsurfing, fishing-trips, tennis; riding sometimes available. Theme buffets: seafood, Creole, Italian, Chinese. Seasonal rates apply. Room service supplement. Expensive.

Le Meridien Fisherman's Cove, PO Box 35, Mahé (tel: 47252). The smaller of two Meridien hotels on Mahé. Traditional granite, timber and palm-thatch rooms. All overlook the sea at the southern end of Beau Vallon Beach. Facilities include a swimming-pool and tennis courts. European/American and Creole music in the evening. International cuisine. Popular with up-market tourists and French visitors. About 10 minutes' drive from Victoria. Expensive.

Northolme Hotel, PO Box 333, Mahé (tel: 47222). The 'Old Northolme' was one of the world's most engaging hotels. Writers loved its rustic ambience. The view is unchanged, but Northolme now has 19 comfortable, air-conditioned rooms and evening entertainment. The Diving Centre enjoys an excellent reputation. 'Funcard' applies (see page 44). Beau Vallon Bay is 20 minutes' walk. Expensive.

Plantation Club, PO Box 437, Victoria, Mahé (tel: 71588). At Val Mer, just outside Baie Lazare village, on the west coast of Mahé (Victoria is about 40 minutes' drive over Sans Souci). 206 rooms and suites, each with mini-bar and television. Vast manicured gardens behind palm-lined beach. Swimming-pool, shop, hairdressing-salon, conference rooms and casino... could be anywhere in the world. All on one level so could be the best place to stay for older tourists. Expensive.

Reef Hotel, PO Box 388, Mahé (tel: 76251). One of Mahé's original tourist hotels, the 150-room Reef is army-barracks style. Every room overlooks the lagoon at Anse aux Pins, 15 minutes' drive from the airport. Despite its unprepossessing appearance, the Reef has many repeat visitors. The atmosphere is relaxed and it is ideal for a night, or two, after island-hopping. The Crafts Village (see page 35) is a 20-minute walk. Swimming-pool, tennis and golf-course; shop; Travel Services Seychelles, Mason's Travel and National Travel Agency desks; and evening

The Reef Hotel at Anse aux Pins on Mahé has fine tennis courts

entertainment. End rooms are quiet. 'Funcard' applies. Expensive.

Seychelles Sheraton, PO Box 540, Mahé (tel: 78541). The Sheraton is an unattractive, block-style hotel set in extensive gardens at Port Glaud. It has 173 air-conditioned rooms with terraces overlooking the Indian Ocean. Local sports include tennis and squash. Arrangements can be made for game-fishing trips. There is a diving centre on Île Thérèse, a 20-minute boat-trip. Thérèse has a beautiful white sand beach which is protected from wind during June–September. L'Islette is off shore about one mile (1.5km) along the coast road (see page 38). The road journey from Victoria to Port Glaud takes about 45 minutes. Expensive.

Sunset Beach, PO Box 372, Glacis, Mahé (tel: 47227). This is one of the world's most romantic hotels on one of the most beautiful beaches in Seychelles. 25 air-conditioned rooms all with a sea view. Outdoor terrace-bar and snacks. Breakfast buffet includes champagne. Popular with honeymooners, the hotel offers a full wedding service. Children under 10 are not allowed. Attractive swimming pool and beach swimming. About 20 minutes' drive from Victoria. Moderate–expensive.

Vista Bay, PO Box 622, Mahé (tel: 47351). One of Mahé's original hotels. 33 air-conditioned apartments recently modernised. All have television and a mini-bar.

Swimming pool. On a hillside with spectacular views, around 30 minutes' drive from Victoria. Moderate.

Guests staying at establishments owned by **Seychelles Hotels** (Beau-Vallon Bay, Northolme, Reef and Vacoa Village on Mahé) are eligible for a free 'Funcard'. The voucher entitles the holder to one free introductory dive between 08.00–09.00 hrs and 20 per cent off other dives and equipment hire. Discount applies to all motorised watersports. Free windsurfing, sailing and canoeing. Other discounts include 10 per cent off scenic flights and car-rental with Mason's Travel, and 10 per cent off excursions to Frégate and Praslin. Certain souvenir shops discount goods on production of the 'Funcard'. It can also be used in the Beau-Vallon Bay Casino – SR50 complimentary on the first SR100 you spend. The card may be exchanged with facilities at any Seychelles Hotels.

Guesthouses

It is impossible to mention all the guesthouses on Mahé. The following list is a selection of the most popular:

Auberge Louis XVII, PO Box 607, La Louise, Mahé (tel: 44411). Situated in a secluded garden site about three miles (5km) up Chemin La Misère, south of Victoria. Transport is essential as the nearest beach is 30 minutes' drive and Victoria is a long steep walk. Twin-bed rooms,

air-conditioning, mini-bar and television. Swimming-pool. Popular with long-stay expatriates. Continental and Creole meals.

The *auberge* is named after the son of Louis XVI and Marie-Antoinette who escaped to Mahé during the French Revolution. He lived under the name of Poiret until his death in 1856, when his true identity was revealed. Cheap–moderate.

Beau Vallon Bungalows, Beau Vallon, Mahé (tel: 47382). Family-run hotel near the Coral Strand at Beau Vallon Beach with eight basic rooms set back from the road. Convenient to local watersports and supermarket. Own bar. Pleasant, but can be noisy (dogs, radio, television). Thieves can slide a hand in the louvred windows so leave nothing within reach. Young tourists like the casual

Harbour View guesthouse, Mahé

atmosphere. Cheap.

Château d'Eau, PO Box 689, Mahé (tel: 78577). Classified as a hotel-restaurant, it has five large, airy rooms with balconies overlooking the sea, at Barbarons on the west coast. Highly recommended to anyone who wishes to avoid mainstream tourism. Very quiet except Sunday lunchtime when it is packed with locals – always a good indication of the food: grilled fish, lobster, crab. Mainly Creole seafood; licensed. Swimming and other watersports at Barbarons Beach. Car essential – Victoria 40 minutes' drive. Right turn, easily missed, near a large coconut plantation. Airport transfers. Moderate.

Harbour View, PO Box 631, Mont Fleuri, Mahé (tel: 22473). Seven large, comfortable rooms in an old waterfront house about 15 minutes' walk from Victoria. Run by a warm Seychelloise, it has good atmosphere. On the bus route and 15 minutes' drive to Seychelles International Airport. Excursions can be arranged. Creole meals. Cheap.

La Résidence Bougainville, PO Box 378, Mahé (tel: 71334). You must stay at least a night in this charming old plantation house. Rooms are small, but the atmosphere is what you come for. Polished wood veranda with sea view, bar and pretty licensed restaurant. Well run, friendly service. Transport essential – 40 minutes' drive from Victoria. Nearest swimming at Anse Royale. A good base from which to visit south Mahé. Cheap.

Manresa, Anse Étoile, Mahé (tel: 41388). Five smallish rooms with balconies and views of Sainte Anne. Relaxed

La Résidence Bougainville, Mahé

atmosphere with pleasant garden-style bar-restaurant. Family TV. Transport useful – about 30 minutes' drive to the nearest swimming beach. Inland walks. Cheap.

North Point Guesthouse, Fonds des Liane, Mahé (tel: 41339). Family-run accommodation in a quiet corner of northwest Mahé. Transport useful, but on a bus route. About 20 minutes' walk to the nearest swimming beach. Beau Vallon watersports centre is 15 minutes' drive. Suitable for younger tourists. Special weekly rates. Simple and cheap.

Panorama Guesthouse, Mare Anglaise, Mahé (tel: 47300). Pleasant small hotel with eight basic rooms. Front rooms overlook the coast road passing Beau Vallon. Well situated: three minutes' walk from the beach and watersports. On a bus route: Victoria 20 minutes. Gloomy restaurant serves Creole food.

Good service from all-women staff. Popular – bookings essential. Cheap.

Pension Bel-Air, PO Box 116, Mahé (tel: 24416). Seven basic rooms in an old colonial-style house on the corner of a busy road above Victoria (about six minutes' uphill climb from the town). Bar and restaurant. Children aged 3-6 at 50 per cent of single adult rate. Cheap–moderate.

Sunrise Guesthouse, PO Box 615, Victoria, Mahé (tel: 24560). Set back from the main road at Mont Fleuri, 20 minutes' walk to Victoria. Family-run small hotel with seven smallish, air-conditioned rooms. Good for a night before your international flight, as the airport is only 15 minutes' drive. Nearest swimming, Anse aux Pins. Cheap.

Villas and Apartments
If you prefer the independence of self catering, Mahé has:

Bel Ombre Holiday Villas, PO Box 528, Bel Ombre, Mahé (tel: 47616). Two bungalows just off the beach at Bel Ombre.

Blue Lagoon, PO Box 442, Anse à la Mouche, Mahé (tel: 71197). Four two-bedroomed bungalows overlooking the sea at Anse à la Mouche.

Michel Holiday Apartments, PO Box 277, Le Rocher, Mahé (tel: 22540). 16 air-conditioned apartments on the outskirts of Victoria. A daily maid service is provided.

Vacoa Village, PO Box 401, Mahé (tel: 47130). The 'village' consists of nine 'Spanish-style' apartments in landscaped grounds at Beau Vallon Bay. There is a swimming pool and a bar.

Nightlife and Entertainment
Tourist hotels on Mahé have nightly entertainment for guests and visitors. The **Equator** at Grand'Anse has a disco and 'folklore' entertainment, and **Auberge Club des Seychelles** at Bel Ombre is recommended for its Seychellois singing and dancing shows. The **Coca Cabana Nightclub** in the Sheraton swings until dawn, while the **Beau Vallon** and **Coral Strand** have nightly music, dancing and limbo competitions. The Seychelles *contredanse* and the *séga* (see page 99–100) are featured by artists in Thursday's cabaret night at the **Meridien Barbarons**. The **Reef Hotel** at Anse aux Pins has loud live music until midnight. Saturdays at the Reef attract many local dancers. You can also catch Seychellois rhythms at the nearby **Ty-Foo**. It is not necessary to dress up although you look silly dancing the *séga* in shorts.

Nightclubs and Discos
The **Katiolo** is a colourful Creole-style nightclub at Anse Faure, 10 minutes' drive from the Reef Hotel. The **Barrel Discothèque** on Revolution Avenue in Victoria has Thursday-Sunday dancing from 21.00-03.00hrs. On the airport road, the modern **Flamboyant** has strobe lighting and exciting music.

Casinos

Mahé has two casinos – at the Beau-Vallon Bay Hotel and the Plantation Club. More central, the former is open 19.00-03.00hrs. Shorts are not permitted after 20.00hrs. Seychellois croupiers are slick dealers. There are five blackjack tables and four roulette wheels: stakes start at SR10 and SR5. You get a concession with a Seychelles Hotels 'Funcard' (see page 44) in the Beau-Vallon Bay Casino which has a convivial ambience for amateur gamblers. Credit cards accepted for bets, but drinks must be paid for in cash. The Plantation Club Casino is possibly more chic. Seychellois are not allowed in either place.

Evening Cruise

Travel Agents operate evening excursions off Mahé by romantic, square-rigged schooners. The cruise leaves Victoria Harbour for Beau Vallon Bay via Northeast Point and anchors off Round Island for a Creole Barbecue and entertainment.

Restaurants

The following are some of the best known restaurants on Mahé. Some hotel restaurants are mentioned under **Hotels** (above).

Beau-Vallon Bay Hotel Pizzeria, (tel: 47167). In the hotel garden, it serves excellent seafood pizzas and other types of pizza.

Beau Vallon Beach Pub & Pizzeria. At the north end of Beau Vallon Bay. Pizza and toasted sandwiches.

Islander Restaurant (tel: 71289). American owned tourist-type restaurant, at Anse La Mouche. Daily specials served. Good clam chowder.

Katiolo Restaurant (tel: 76453). Bar-disco with small seaside restaurant at Anse Faure, about 10 minutes from Seychelles International Airport. Creole-type menu reasonably priced. Open 19.00hrs. for dinner.

Kaz Creole (tel: 71680). At Anse Royale. Pleasant location on the beach. Ambitious French-style cuisine and local dishes. Chateaubriand a speciality. Good wine-list. Genial Seychellois-South African owners. Lunch and dinner served. Also morning tea or coffee. Expensive.

Kyoto Restaurant (tel: 41337). Set back off the main road at Anse Étoile north of Victoria. Japanese cuisine.

La Marmite (tel: 22932). Creole restaurant in central Victoria. Moderate prices.

La Perle Noir (tel: 47046). Convenient for Beau Vallon. Extensive menu with many Creole dishes: stuffed clams; baked kingfish; palm-heart salad; smoked swordfish; plus Continental meals. The best service in Seychelles. Free courtesy bus by arrangement.

La Sirene (tel: 71339). Speciality seafood restaurant at Anse aux Poules Bleues, southwest Mahé. Nice for lunch. Good fish soup.

Le Corsaire (tel: 47171). Very attractive waterfront restaurant at Bel Ombre offering up-market dining. Good, imaginative French-style cooking: seafood cream soup with aubergine and garlic; love apple mousse with prawns and tarragon sauce; lobster fricassee with noodles; lamb saddle in puff pastry; hot coconut tart; chilled nougat and fruit coulis. Expensive.

Lobster Pot (tel: 41376). At Pointe Conan, north Mahé – about 15 minutes' drive from Victoria. A simple restaurant on the waterfront overlooking Sainte Anne Marine National Park. Variety of good seafood dishes from octopus salad (reasonable price) to lobster thermidor (expensive). Well run by Miss Leonie Benoiton. Lunch especially recommended. You will probably return.

Marie-Antoinette Restaurant (tel: 23942). At the top of Revolution Avenue in Victoria. A charming old plantation house, beautifully decorated by patron Madame Fonseka. The same menu has been served for 16 years: *tec-tec*; lentil or pumpkin soup; parrot fish in butter; aubergine salad; chicken curry; fresh fruit salad; banana caramel, etc. No à la carte. Open daily for lunch and dinner (except on Sunday). Reservations essential. Your best chance of trying typical cooking at a moderate price.

Pomme Canelle (tel: 76155). In Le Village Artisanal. Beautiful plantation-style house. Extensive Creole menu features traditional dishes found nowhere else in Seychelles. Examples: fruit bat with red wine; breadfruit soup;

Kitchen of the Marie-Antoinette Restaurant in Victoria

ginger crab and grilled fish in lime sauce. Easy parking. Bookings essential on Friday or Saturday. Open for lunch. Expensive but worth trying.

Scala Restaurant (tel: 47535). Situated at Bel Ombre. Italian and Creole specialities; fish soup; stuffed clams; home-made pasta. Also excellent steaks. Espresso coffee. Pleasant ambience. Open weekdays from 19.00hrs; closed on Sunday.

Ty-Foo Restaurant (tel: 71485). At La Plaine. 15 minutes' drive from the airport. Chinese and Creole cooking. Busy on Saturday nights. Disco.

The Hotel School restaurant (Bel Ombre road). Open daily 12.00-14.00hrs. and Wednesday and Friday 19.00-21.30hrs. Moderate.

Snacks

There are no Western-type snack-bars in Seychelles, and Victoria may also be the only capital without a Kentucky Fried Chicken. Hamburgers, sandwiches and other snacks are sold at the **Pirate's Arms**, a popular licensed rendezvous on Independence Avenue. In the adjacent lane, **Le Boucanier** sells boring boxed take-aways (tuna fricassee; pork stew). **King Wah** on Benezet Street sells equally bland Chinese take-aways. A hole-in-the-wall in Victoria Arcade sells dried-out samosas and other take-away food.

Shopping

Mahé is the only island in Seychelles for serious shoppers. You can buy T-shirts, shorts and swimwear with eye-catching local designs in Victoria's boutiques (also in hotel shops). Look for the label 'Sunstroke Designs' – their retail outlet is outside the open market in Victoria.

O Trouloulou, a boutique next to the popular bar 'The Pirate's Arms' on Independence Avenue, stocks local gear. The street stalls on Independence Avenue are good for browsing. A popular buy is a sarong to wear over your swimming costume.

For souvenirs:
Le Village Artisanal (see page 35), near the Reef Hotel. Striking Seychelles-style garments can also be bought here. Tel: 76100.
Macouti Curio Shop at Beau Vallon (tel: 47043). *Open:*

Monday to Saturday 09.00-17.00hrs.

For something different:
La Marine Model Boat Centre (see page 35), near Le Village Artisanal. Prices of models range from SR28,000, including expert packing on the premises – not for the limited budget. Tel: 71441.
Seychelles Creations (tel: 21516). Situated at Le Rocher, 15 minutes' drive south along the coast from Victoria, this is a government co-operative making buttons and jewellery from the iridescent green snail-shell. *Chiocciola verde*. When polished, the shell becomes a lustrous mother-of-pearl, at one time a major export. You are welcome to visit the factory, which makes key-rings and other curios, as well as sets of buttons. You can buy beautiful sets of pearl buttons, which would cost three to four times as much at home.
Open: Monday to Friday 08.00-12.00 and 13.00-16.00hrs. Closed Saturday and Sunday.

For teas, spices and perfumes:
Kreolfleurage (see page 34) at Northeast Point (tel: 41329). Local floral essences are sold here.
Tea Tavern (see page 37) on the Chemin Sans Souci sells a variety of teas.
Victoria Market – JA Adriene (see page 97) sells spices, essences and chutneys.

Teas and spices are also sold in the duty-free shop at Mahé International Airport.

PRASLIN

The usual pattern for tourists has been to visit Praslin from Mahé. However, preferring to start their visit in the quieter environment of Praslin, increasing numbers of people are now doing the reverse. A large, granitic island, Praslin is most famous for the Vallée de Mai National Park. Watersports and interisland boat-trips are also popular and there are many trail walks. You need a car to explore properly: Praslin measures seven miles (11km) by five miles (8km), with a central mountain ridge covered in luxuriant vegetation. The coast is characterised by many caves and granite rocks. You can also get around by bicycle.

Anse Volbert at Côte d'Or is the most developed tourist centre. Elsewhere remains rustic.

Praslinois number around 5,000. Farming, fishing and tourism provide the main employment. Vanilla and copra used to be important crops, but disease killed the vanilla vines and copra became too costly. Plantations still stretch as far as the eye can see. Tropical fruits such as mangoes, limes, passionfruit and melons flourish in the hot, moist climate. Grand'Anse in the southwest is an important guava-growing district. Praslin has a good water supply and excellent communications. You can call anywhere direct with a phone-card at Cable and Wireless (Grand'Anse) or Praslin airport. Local settlements are linked by a good, sealed road.

Getting There

Air Seychelles operates 26 regular flights a day to Praslin and back to Mahé. A booking is useful in peak holiday time. Otherwise roll up and buy a ticket at the Interisland Airport. For details see **Directory** page 121. The 15-

Shop at Grand'Anse, Praslin

minute hop allows good views of Sainte Anne Marine National Park off Mahé. Praslin Airport is small but adequate with a WC and shop selling souvenirs – do not buy turtle shell (see page 97).

For the return journey, either go to the airport and make a booking in person, or call Mahé airport to make your reservation (tel: 73101). You cannot call Praslin Airport to make a reservation.

If you prefer to travel by sea, there is a regular ferry service between Praslin and Mahé – see **Directory** page 122 for details.

Getting About

A car – ideally a 'Mini-Moke' or a four-wheel drive vehicle like a Suzuki jeep – is essential

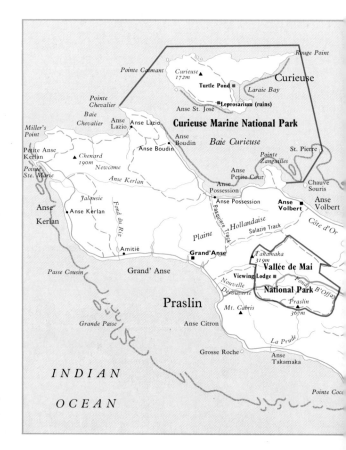

to explore thoroughly. You will need at least three to four days. If you are short of time take Mason's Travel's full-day island excursion which includes hotel pick-up, lunch and a visit to the Vallée de Mai.

Bicycles may be rented at Côte d'Or. See also **Directory** page 121 for information on buses and taxis.

PRASLIN

```
0         1         2 km
0              1 mile
```

Anse
Matelot

nse
ouvernement *Fond Diable*
            213m ▲   Grand Anse
              • Au Cap   • Anse La Blague
            Anse   Petite Anse
      Anse Takamaka
     Madge   *Au Morne*   *Pointe*
                              La
ie   *Farine*
e. Anne *Baie*
        Ste. Anne   Anse La Farine
     Anse
    L'Amour
                              Île Ronde

              Pointe Cabris

nse
arie-Louise
     • Anse Marie-Louise
• Anse Consolation
      Pointe Consolation
 Anse
Consolation

WHAT TO SEE

◆◆◆
ANSE CONSOLATION DRIVE
southeast coast
The road from Grand'Anse around Pointe Consolation to Baie Sainte Anne is rough in places, but it is a beautiful drive to be enjoyed slowly. There are plans to tar the road, but import of tarmacadam is difficult, as it can only be unloaded on a high tide at the Baie Sainte Anne jetty. Lunch at Les Rochers Restaurant is recommended (see page 60) or take a picnic. Beyond Grosse Roche are small bays with good snorkelling. **Anse Takamaka** is pretty, with cane fish-traps stacked under the trees. There is a beach at Anse Marie-Louise beyond Pointe Consolation. Non-stop, the circuit takes about 40 minutes.

Cane fish traps on Praslin

PRASLIN

◆◆◆
ANSE LAZIO
northwest coast

The background scenes in *Castaway*, the movie of Lucy Irvine's desert-island book, were mainly filmed at Anse Lazio. A dazzling white sand beach lined with *takamaka* trees, it is an all-day walk from Côte d'Or. The road follows the coast past fishermen's huts and secluded bays. Anse Lazio is a great spot for lovers, families and thieves. Leave nothing of value on the beach. A nearby store sells soft drinks and shells. It is a wonderful place for a picnic.

La Réserve Hotel, Praslin

◆◆◆
ANSE VOLBERT (Côte d'Or)
northeast coast

A good concrete-faced road slices across the 'neck' of Praslin from Anse Madge to the Côte d'Or, as this stretch of shore is known. Anse Volbert is a long sweep of beach ideal for all watersports. Praslin's main watersports centre is located within the grounds of the Praslin Beach Hotel here. Most of the main tourist hotels are built back in the trees; others have private beaches. You can visit **Christine Harter's art gallery**, next to the Village du Pêcheur hotel.
Bicycles may be hired locally. Boats go to **Chauve Souris Island**, visible from Anse Volbert. Good swimming; lunch at the island lodge.

◆◆◆
BAIE SAINTE ANNE
east coast

The lovely Baie Sainte Anne is your first sight of Praslin on arrival by boat from Mahé (sailing time is normally three hours). New shops are being built in Baie Sainte Anne village, though it is likely to remain quiet. At time of writing it had a string of little stores, a hospital, a church and Barclays Bank (open 08.30-12.00hrs, five days). Tour buses, taxis and rent-a-car representatives meet the boat. The best idea is to negotiate a 'Mini Moke' on the spot. Sainte Anne is 12 minutes' drive from the Côte d'Or and about 15 minutes, via the Vallée de Mai National Park, from Grand'Anse.

♦
GRAND'ANSE
southwest coast
This is the biggest village on
Praslin. It has an Indian-run
general store, several
boutiques, a bank (the Banque
Française Commerciale), a
church, Cable and Wireless
station and the fish market.
Near here is the much
photographed **Seychelles
Independence Monument**
featuring the erotic coco-de-
mer. There are several
pleasant hotels on Grand'Anse
and a good beach, but the
lagoon is too shallow for
enjoyable swimming. The
Maison des Palmes hotel near
Praslin Airport has a small
swimming pool (see page 59).
You can take a boat-trip to
Cousin, from Grand'Anse (see
page 67).

*Pointe Sainte Marie with the
poignant grave of a drowned child*

♦♦♦
POINTE SAINTE MARIE
west coast
It is 15 minutes' drive from
Grand'Anse to Pointe Sainte
Marie. If you take the public
bus, it goes to the farm. Follow
the track through the coconut
plantation. **Anse Kerlan** is a
good bathing beach, **Petite
Anse Kerlan** even better. But
watch the currents: the grave
and the statue of Sainte Marie
on the bluff are in memory of a
child who drowned here. It is
an easy climb to the headland
from where you can enjoy a
good view.
Allow half a day for the trip
and take a picnic. The bus
back to Grand'Anse leaves
every 40 minutes.

◆◆◆
VALLÉE DE MAI NATIONAL PARK
central Praslin

When General Gordon of Khartoum fame visited Praslin, he compared the Vallée de Mai to the Garden of Eden. If anywhere deserves this accolade, it is this amazing, primeval plant world, only 15 minutes' drive from either Côte d'Or or Grand'Anse.

Until the 1930s, the Vallée de Mai was virtually untouched by man, but during the next decade there was a good deal of logging and a number of fires. In an attempt to repair the damage, many ornamental or exotic shrubs were planted. The plan now, however, is to encourage the establishment of original native palm forest. Responsibility for this rests with the National Parks and Nature Conservation Commission of the Seychelles. It is easy to find your way around the Vallée de Mai using the official brochure, which also lists the plants and wildlife in the reserve. Paths are well signposted and not too steep: a fit elderly person could manage the Circular Walk.

The entrance to the park is flanked by coco-de-mer palms (see **Peace and Quiet** page 88) and several good examples of vacoa parasol screwpines. Follow the signs: at the first left-hand fork there is a huge jackfruit tree, an exotic from Asia. Look closely if you have never seen one: the huge yellow fruits grow straight out of its trunk. Further

on is a *bois rouge* tree covered with South American aroid. A popular household plant, similar to the arum lily, it is a spreading invader in the park's hot, moist climate.

The clump of coco-de-mer palms near Sign 2 probably goes back more than a thousand years. The tallest, estimated at 32 feet (10m), could have germinated from a nut about the time of the first settlement in Seychelles in the 18th century. Beyond here the valley contains one of the best developed mixed palm forests in the islands. Stand still and listen to the eerie sound made by the giant palm fronds rubbing together in the wind. The screech you might take to be the rare black parrot is more likely a mynah bird imitating its call. Bronze

Vallée de Mai: coco-de-mer palms

geckos – *mangouya* in Creole – rustle the carpet of leaves. A patient wait by the small stream might reveal some shrimps.

For a general panorama of the Vallée de Mai follow the trail on your map. The upper slopes are drier and vegetation is less luxuriant compared with below. Following the trail again, you will see a huge granite mass near Sign 6. It dates from the Precambrian era and is estimated to be around 650 million years old. When you reach the park seat, note the lofty coco-de-mer on your right. Measured at 101 feet (31m), it is the tallest in the valley.

Valley open to visitors: daily 08.30-17.30hrs.

Entrance charge includes a pamphlet with walking trails. Allow two to three hours. For photography, midday is best with the sun overhead, but you will still require flash in the shadowy undergrowth. At times the leaf canopy is so thick it is dark. (Take note of the sign that says: 'Take only photographs – leave only footprints'.)

Other Walks
Secluded bays and forest trails make Praslin ideal to explore on foot. You could try:
Salazie Track from Côte d'Or, just along from the Praslin Beach and Village du Pêcheur hotels, across the island to Grand'Anse, finishing near the church.
Pasquiere Track, which branches off the Salazie Track behind Grand'Anse, and continues to Anse Possession.
Anse Volbert to Anse Matelot via the **east coast** track.
Anse Madge (on Baie Sainte Anne) to **Petite Anse**, via Anse Takamaka, a walk across Praslin's easternmost promontory.

Excursions
Interisland Ferry to La Digue.
This is a 30-minute trip by comfortable motor-yacht. Daily departures from Sainte Anne jetty at 07.00, 09.30, 10.30, 14.30, 17.00hrs (no 09.30hrs sailing on Sunday). Return from La Digue jetty: 07.30, 10.00, 11.30, 15.30, 17.30hrs (no 10.00hrs sailing on Sunday).
Island Excursions to Cousin, Curieuse, St Pierre and Aride are bookable through all hotels and travel agents.

PRASLIN

Accommodation

Praslin has some stunning hotels and several small guesthouses, bookable locally. There is likely to be a room shortage during peak holiday periods so reserve in advance. Choose the location of your hotel carefully. During the southeast trades when Grand'Anse is choked by brown seaweed, Côte d'Or is relatively clear and protected from wind. The reverse is true during November to February.

Beach Villa Guesthouse, Grand'Anse, Praslin (tel: 33445). This is a small, eight-room, family-run hotel owned by a retired Seychelles civil servant. His daughter, Marie-France, is in charge. Tariff includes full English breakfast, in your room or in a round-house behind the beach. Other meals are prepared on request. Rooms are simple, but pleasant, and spotlessly clean. There is swimming at high tide on Grand'Anse beach. Fishing trips and excursions are bookable through the hotel. Ten minutes' drive from Praslin Airport, within strolling distance of local stores, and near the Coco Bello Nightclub and the Banque Française Commerciale. Children under three free. Cheap.

Britannia Guesthouse, Grand'Anse, Praslin (tel: 33215). Ten minutes from Praslin Airport and located up a quiet road within walking distance of stores in Grand'Anse. Lies well back from Grand'Anse beach. This is a homely place with clean, basic rooms. Good set meals with generous portions. Restaurant open to non-residents. Cheap.

Flying Dutchman, Grand'Anse, Praslin (tel: 33337). Bungalow-style hotel owned by Seychelles Hotels, five minutes from Praslin Airport and within walking distance of local shops. The hotel is divided in two by the coast road around Praslin. The restaurant, bar, shop and office are on Grand'Anse beachfront; bungalows, set back from the road, sleep 36 in total. Quiet, but basic.

Saturday half-day deep-sea fishing trips are bookable – depart 06.00hrs. Seychelles Hotels 'Funcard' discount (see page 44). Moderate.

Indian Ocean Fishing Club, Grand'Anse, Praslin (tel: 33324). One of the originals on Praslin, recently refurbished to provide luxury accommodation. Beachfront location, near the Flying Dutchman. Specialises in fishing. Moderate–expensive.

La Réserve, Anse Petite Cour, Praslin (tel: 32211). Twelve large bungalows in a gorgeous location on Anse Petite Cour (north coast), 30 minutes from Praslin Airport. Good tennis courts, snorkelling and fishing. Diving and other excursions arranged by the Watersports Centre in the Praslin Beach Hotel, 10 minutes' walk away. Transport – jeeps, cars, bicycles, taxis – can be arranged. Good à la carte meals in an enchanting jetty-style restaurant. French, Creole, Chinese menu; barbecues. Highly recommended for privacy. Ideal for jaded business people. Younger visitors find it too quiet, but Côte d'Or hotels are near by. Expensive.

L'Archipel, Anse Gouvernement, Praslin (tel: 32242). Elegant, up-market hotel in 19 acres (8 hectares) of tropical gardens. The 16 large, extremely comfortable rooms overlook a private, north-facing beach. Windsurfing, canoeing and snorkelling are included in the room rate. Bicycles can be hired. Transport is essential as the hotel is 20 minutes' drive from Praslin Airport and it is a long walk to Vallée de Mai, or Côte d'Or. Open upstairs restaurant; menu includes Creole specialities – pumpkin cream soup, palm-heart gratinée, red snapper fillet, etc. Owner, Louis d'Offay, is from a former 'Grand Blanc' family in Seychelles. Many guests are European honeymooners. Men are required to wear trousers at dinner. Very expensive.

Maison des Palmes, Amitié, Praslin (tel: 33411). This is a pleasant, moderate-sized hotel on the southwest coast, two minutes from the airport. Its 16 thatched bungalows, set in a garden of palms and frangipani on Grand'Anse are large, clean and comfortable. Good swimming at high tide. Seaweed and sandflies are a problem during the southeast trades. Nice bar, restaurant and small swimming-pool. 15 minutes by bus, or car from the Vallée de Mai. All excursions on Praslin can be booked through hotel reception.

Foliage on Praslin

Departure point for Cousin. Moderate.

Orange-Tree Guesthouse, Baie Sainte Anne, Praslin (tel: 33248). Five very basic rooms high up a steep drive, far from anywhere except the ferry jetty to La Digue – 25 minutes' drive from Praslin Airport, and miles from any restaurant (B/B only). Transport is essential unless you are very fit. Cheap.

Paradise Hotel, Anse Volbert, Praslin (tel: 32255). This hotel is well located at Côte d'Or, one of the best beaches on Praslin. It consists of 21 very spacious, thatch-roofed bungalows set in well manicured grounds. Popular with both young and older tourists, it is one of the best package hotels in Seychelles. Good, international-style meals. Lively bi-weekly Creole cabaret-buffet; barbecues.

Travel agents have a desk for excursions. Attractive coastal walks. Other beach hotels are five minutes away on foot. The airport is 25 minutes away by taxi.

Owned by Paradise Resorts, highly recommended for families with children. Moderate–expensive.

Praslin Beach Hotel, Anse Volbert, Praslin (tel: 32222). Large Hotel on Côte d'Or beach, north Praslin. Owned by Seychelles Hotels so you can use your 'Funcard' (see page 44). Rooms are set around a swimming-pool featuring a sunken bar. Noise is a problem. Staff are jaded as the hotel has a big turnover of package tourists. Shop, tennis and excellent watersports centre. Central location – car not necessary. Take a taxi from Praslin Airport, 25 minutes. Moderate–expensive.

Village du Pêcheur, Anse Volbert, Praslin (tel: 32030). Nine round, thatch-roofed bungalows, clean, but claustrophobic. Pleasant beachfront bar and popular restaurant. Games room, with video cassettes. Children will like it. All excursions can be booked through reception. Best time for the Village du Pêcheur and other Côte d'Or hotels is June-September, when they are sheltered from the wind. Excellent swimming, sunbathing. Moderate.

Restaurants

It is a good idea to take half-board wherever you stay on Praslin. Outside the hotels there are only two or three restaurants, although this is a situation likely to change as the island becomes increasingly popular. The alternative is to take bed and breakfast only. With a car, you can then try various restaurants and hotels.

Les Rochers, (tel: 33230). Located at Grosse Roche on the south coast, this is one of the best restaurants in Seychelles. At present it can only be reached by a rough road, 15 minutes' drive from the Vallée de Mai/Anse Consolation signpost. Daily seafood specialities, good wine list. Open for lunch and dinner. Closed on Sunday.

Laurier, (tel: 32241). Located at Anse Volbert, this is popular with people staying on the Côte d'Or. It is a small, relaxed, bistro-style restaurant, next to the Praslin Beach Hotel, serving unpretentious, Creole-style meals. Licensed; pleasant staff; no 'muzak'. Good for families. Moderate prices. Lunch: 12.30-14.30hrs and dinner 19.30-21.30hrs (last order).

Entertainment and Nightlife

The best entertainment on Praslin is provided by the **Paradise Hotel** which stages a weekly Creole buffet dinner with local dancing. Good family entertainment, it begins at 20.00 hours.

On the last Saturday of every month, the **Coco Bello Nightclub** at Grand'Anse resounds with irresistible rhythms. Convenient for visitors staying at the Beach Villas, Flying Dutchman or Maison des Palmes.

OTHER ISLANDS

ARIDE

Inner Islands
You can smell the bewitching scent of *bois citron* (see below) as you approach Île Aride from Praslin, six miles (10km) to the south.

A granitic island, it was bought for a British wildlife organisation, the Royal Society for Nature Conservation, in 1973, and is second only in importance to Aldabra. It is still managed by the RSNC. Aride is the only site in the world where the *bois citron*, or Wright's gardenia grows. A second species, unique to Aride, is a type of *Peponium*, a plant related to the cucumber although inedible. The island has more breeding sea birds than anywhere else in the archipelago, and six times more insects.

You are taken on a walking tour of the sea bird colonies by a British warden. From the island's highest point, Gros la Tête (443 feet/135m), you can see hundreds of frigatebirds and tropicbirds planing over the sea. Dolphins are also common in local waters.

Getting There

Less than a thousand people a year visit Aride as boat-owners on Praslin usually say the seas are too rough for them to risk the journey.

The island remains open throughout the time of the southeast trades during May to October, but landings are subject to reasonable weather. Usual visiting days are Wednesday, Thursday, Friday and Sunday between 09.00 and 12.00hrs. The boat-owner, or your hotel, will check conditions with Bon Espoir (the Mahé communications centre) at 08.00hrs to see if Aride is open (tel: 76733).

Departures are from Grand'Anse and Côte d'Or on Praslin – sailing time 40-60 minutes. Pack all belongings in a waterproof bag. There is a landing fee as well as the excursion fee. Bookings can be made through TSS and other travel agents.

White-tailed tropicbird

BIRD ISLAND (ÎLE AUX VACHES)

Inner Islands

Many visitors consider a visit here the highlight of a holiday in Seychelles.

The island is officially called Île aux Vaches ('Island of Cows'). This was originally Île aux Vaches Marines after the docile dugongs, or sea-cows, marine mammals which once inhabited these waters but are now sadly rare.

The British called it Bird Island after the millions of sea birds that flock to breed on the island during the southeast trades, and it is now commonly referred to by this name. Early this century the birds' population was so dense that no vegetation could grow. Now the island is clothed with trees.

A flat axe-shaped coral island, only 13 feet (4m) above sea-level, Bird Island is ringed by some of the most spectacular white beaches in the Indian Ocean. About two miles (3km) off shore, the Seychelles Bank drops vertically 6,000 to 6,500 feet (1,800-2,000m): you have a good view of the coral plateau from the aircraft as you arrive or depart.

Development is kept to a minimum – do not go to Bird Island expecting a swimming pool, television or nightlife. Dress is casual: you can lunch in your swimming costume, and there are no dress rules for dinner. The only inhabitants are the staff of the island's sole hotel (see **Accommodation** below), so if you are discreet you can also indulge in some topless sunbathing.

What to See

You can see Bird Island in a day, but its size is deceptive. The island is less than a mile (1,500m) long, but it takes two to three hours to walk around it, as the soft, white beaches are as heavy going as newly fallen snow.

Walking south from Bird Island Lodge (see below) around the end of the airstrip, you reach **Passe Cocos**. Island boats moor here during the trades but anchorages change during the monsoon season. At **Passe Hirondelle**, to the northeast, is the farm, producing most of the island's food requirements – okra, aubergines, melons, pumpkins, limes and peppers, as well as pigs and chickens. Migratory sea birds, mainly sooty terns, are still plentiful. Ornithologists estimate there are between 600,000-800,000 pairs nesting on the island between April and October. The daily plane from Mahé inevitably clips a tern, or two, but the huge colony at the end of the airstrip appears largely unperturbed by aircraft.

There are no rules regarding the island's **tern colony**, as the sooty terns police themselves. They allow you to approach their nests to within 50 feet (15m) – any closer and you risk a pecking. The sight of terns hovering over fleeing bathers is common.

Crudely-built hides enable bird-watching all day. The activity is non-stop, with nesting terns sprinkling sea-

Sooty tern colony on Bird Island

water on the sand to flatten the vegetation. When the chicks hatch, there are constant sorties for shoaling fish.
Other local sea birds are fairy terns, noddys, barred ground doves and an occasional red-capped Madagascar fody. The air is filled with bird-calls and everything – you included if you remain still for long – is splashed with white bird droppings.
The island is also important as a breeding ground for turtles.

Accommodation
Bird Island Lodge, PO Box 404, Victoria, Mahé, (tel: 21525). Staying at Bird Island Lodge is like being in the centre of a giant aviary so if this is likely to cause offence go instead to Île Denis (see page 67). You will, however, miss a unique experience.

Thatch-roofed chalets are built along the beach, on the west side of the island. Beds are comfortable with the world's softest pillows (for blotting out dawn bird-noise). Night sounds are made by crickets and the crashing surf; be careful not to tread on the ghost-crabs. Cooking at the lodge is plain, but excellent. Breakfast is served from 07.30 to 09.30hrs, and a cow-bell, rung vigorously at 13.00 and 20.00hrs, signals lunch and dinner. A typical buffet features grilled swordfish, tuna fricassee, pork *filet*, rice, shredded papaya, grated coconut, and home-grown peppers and pumpkin. Servings are generous and the service is good. There is a twice-weekly evening barbecue. Tea is also served – in a civilised pot as opposed to teabags. Alcoholic beverages are available at the bar.

Indoor entertainment is low-key. Billiards, darts and card-games are available from the office. The hotel library stocks mainly English-language books as 60 per cent of visitors are British.

Outdoor activities are tennis, snorkelling, glass-bottom boat trips (no windsurfing, sailing or water-skiing). Check the fishing when you make a booking as the local fishermen may have gone to Mahé. You need to bring all your gear. Good beach casting is available. Swimming is superb but beware of currents on the northeast coast. Average water temperature is 26-28°C (78-82°F).

Bird Island Lodge is ideal for families, but children must be supervised.

Esmeralda, the world's largest land tortoise, is star entertainer. A male (despite his name), he weighs 705 pounds (320kg), is aged around 150 years and is acknowledged in *The Guinness Book of Records*. How Esmeralda came to Bird Island in the first place is a mystery.

Bird Island Lodge has a small shop, but you should bring everything you need. Credit cards are accepted.

You stay at the hotel under an all-inclusive package deal, which is obligatory.

Getting There

Bird Island is about 60 miles (100km) north of Mahé. Air Seychelles runs daily flights from Mahé (flight time about 30 minutes).

COUSIN AND COUSINE
Inner Islands

Cousin is a nature reserve where everything from birds to millipedes is protected. A highlight for nature-lovers, it lies 1¼ miles (2km) off Grand'Anse, Praslin. Its sister island, Cousine, cannot be visited.

Two decades ago, Cousin's population of Seychelles brush warblers – wren-like birds found nowhere else – was almost extinct. The colony had been decimated at the beginning of this century when the island's natural vegetation was cleared for coconut plantations.

Concerned at the warblers' disappearance, the International Council for Bird Preservation, based in

Cambridge, England, bought Cousin in 1968. Seven years later, the Seychelles government designated it a Special Reserve. From near extinction, the Seychelles brush warbler, or *'petit merle des Îles'* has increased its numbers to more than 400. Covering 66 acres (27 hectares), Cousin is composed of granite, and phosphatic limestone formed over hundreds of years from the guano deposits of nesting sea birds. Temporary freshwater pools are found in a depression at the foot of the hill. The southern axis supports a small mangrove swamp inundated at high tide. Natural vegetation has been allowed to

Cousine viewed from Cousin

flourish so that original bush now predominates.

Among common native trees on Cousin are *bois mapou* or *Pisonia grandis* whose seeds are dispersed by birds; screwpine found among the granite outcrops; tortoise tree or *Morinda citrifolia*, flourishing on the plateau; and Australian casuarina pines, which make popular nesting sites. Castor oil plants, bamboo and cotton are among some 72 species of introduced plants. Visitors, restricted to 20 at a time, are admitted to Cousin on three mornings a week (see **Getting There**, below). Picnics, snorkelling and removing shells (alive, or dead) are forbidden. Swimming is also technically not allowed.

What to See

Beyond the beach where you land, you find yourself in a screeching, seething, rustling mass of birds, crabs and reptile life. Cousin is estimated to have more lizards and skinks per square metre than anywhere else in the world. You are not allowed to wander around the island at will. There are six local wardens, one of whom will lead your 1½-hour walking tour of Cousin, after an introduction in a beach-hut. Note that flashlight photography of nesting birds is forbidden, and the shadowy foliage unfortunately precludes taking good pictures. Flash-guns as well as other possessions can be left in safety in the beach-hut. Gym-boots are recommended for the walk up to the granite hill-

COUSIN AND COUSINE

Cousin giant millipede

top, 226 feet (69m) above sea-level. Children and elderly tourists should be able to manage without much difficulty.

Do not fall over yourself to photograph the first lizard, or skink you see. They are bigger, fatter and equally tame further along the trail. Skinks are the most common of 11 reptiles found on Cousin. The larger, more boldly patterned is Wright's skink. The other, the Seychelles skink, is widely distributed throughout the archipelago. Both are raiders, and where eggs are vulnerable, the wardens build protective cairns around the nests. Ghost-crabs are nocturnal poachers which also attack and eat baby turtles. The skinks and crabs do, however, keep Cousin clean of carcasses.

On the nature walk the guide may point out a marsh terrapin in the swamp. From the leafy carpet he can pick out an aggressive, but non-poisonous whip scorpion or, reaching under a shady rock, a giant millipede. This harmless vegetarian roams Cousin at night, when bats from Praslin come to feast on figs and mangoes.

Birdlife

Cousin is an important breeding site for sea birds and other birds. You will see a greater variety of birds here – at close range and against varied backgrounds – than on Bird Island.

The Seychelles brush warbler's trilling song is usually heard before you spot the tiny bird, hopping and fluttering in the foliage. It can only fly about 300 feet (100m), which is why it used to be unique to Cousin (there are now colonies on Aride and Cousine).

Other birds are the common brown noddy, which builds a scruffy nest, and the delicate, though lazy, fairy tern which builds no nest at all. She lays a single egg on a branch and sits on this precarious site until it hatches. The chick remains on the bough for 28 days before risking its wings.

Climbing the hill, you can hear the spooky moaning of wedge-tail shearwaters on their nests in the rocks. White-tailed tropicbirds make a spectacular sight on the wing against the turquoise ocean. Other species are the Madagascar fody, the Seychelles sunbird and the barred ground dove.

Cousin supports over 200,000 pairs of breeding sea birds of seven different species (see also **Peace and Quiet**).

COUSIN AND COUSINE/CURIEUSE/DENIS

Getting There

Mason's Travel on Praslin arranges a pick-up and transfer to the boat for Cousin: departure from Grand'Anse at 09.00hrs on Tuesday, Thursday and Friday. Return is at 12.30hrs. A landing fee is payable.

You travel by speedboat or motor-yacht. Off Cousin you disembark into a rubber dinghy. Easily beached, a rubber boat also prevents the accidental introduction of rats which would prove catastrophic for wildlife. Travel agents on Praslin also organise a 'Trois Îles' tour, visiting Curieuse and St Pierre, as well as Cousin. Bookings can be made through your hotel or travel agent on Praslin. Take everything you may require as there are no shops or hotels. A barbecue lunch is included in the cost. Snorkelling gear is provided. Remember to protect your camera in a waterproof bag. Trips are sometimes cancelled during rough seas (June–August).

Facilities

Soft drinks (but no snacks) are available in the beach-hut. There is a basic WC.

Cousine

Cousine, to the southwest of Cousin, was neglected by its former owners. Now cleared of cats which had ravaged birdlife, it supports a colony of Seychelles brush warblers established by wardens from Cousin in 1990. The island remains closed to visitors, but you have a good view of it from the hill-top on Cousin.

CURIEUSE

Inner Islands
A channel one mile (1,500m) wide separates Praslin from Curieuse, which until 1965 was a leper colony. Ten people live there, including the custodian of a colony of giant land tortoises brought here from Aldabra. The plan in putting tortoises on Curieuse was to make these fascinating reptiles more accessible to visitors, but of the original trans-migrants, only about 80 remain. Poached in the night, Aldabra tortoises have popped up all over Seychelles. Curieuse is designated a Marine National Park. A barrier across Laraie Bay protects a turtle colony. There are several trail-walks along Anse St José bay on the south coast. You can see the old leper colony, established in 1833, and an old Creole house used by the doctor who visited from Praslin.

Getting There

Curieuse is visited from Praslin on the 'Trois Îles' tour (see under **Cousin**).

DENIS

Inner Islands
Île Denis is one of the best kept secrets in the Indian Ocean. A coral island 50 miles (80km) north of Mahé, it was claimed by Denis de Trobriand, skipper of *L'Etoile*, who landed there on 11 August 1773 on a voyage to Pondicherry in India. The present owner is Pierre Burckhardt, a retired French industrialist. A benign dictator,

DENIS

Burckhardt once sent a letter to the Seychelles government proposing an independent Republic of Denis. The island already has its own rules – even Denis Time (one hour ahead of the rest of Seychelles).

Denis is a glorious escape from life's travails, but it will not suit everyone. Poseurs will hate it as there is no stage. People with a low boredom level may go bananas. And single women are viewed with suspicion: reservations for Denis Island Lodge (see **Accommodation** below) are not taken without a background check!

What to See

Denis has one village, whose houses line a track known as the Champs Élysées. Most of the 60 locals are involved in farming and fishing. Many also work at Denis Island Lodge. The 'old village' is found on the north side of the airstrip. You can visit the island farm and watch copra being processed – usually on Wednesday at 17.00hrs. Near here is the island lighthouse; the original was raised in 1881. You may see the inevitable giant land tortoise plodding up the Champs Élysées. Otherwise there is no traffic on Denis. Note the small white chapel and cemetery beyond the last house on the right. It takes about 2½ hours to circumambulate the island at low tide: check the tide-chart posted outside the hotel boutique. You can walk along the beach above sea-level, but

take shoes for rocky spots. Sea birds are rare, but crabs scuttle out of your way. Coral fish are seen trapped in pools. Swimming, especially on the lodge side, is glorious.

Accommodation

Denis Island Lodge, PO Box 404, Victoria, Mahé, (tel: 44143).

You stay in huge, well-spaced bungalows under shady trees behind the beach. There is oodles of space in the bathroom with bath, shower and separate bidet and WC. The hotel is run with great understatement – the policy is to treat clients as house-guests. You must dress for dinner, but you can go barefoot. The atmosphere is relaxed; staff are friendly and efficient. Beds are turned down – rare in Seychelles – and a mosquito coil is lit at sunset.

A full British breakfast is served from 07.30 to 09.30hrs. An excellent Creole lunch-buffet features at least four main courses, cool tropical salads and half a dozen different tarts, puddings and fruits. The hotel is fully licensed: bar times 10.00-15.00 and 17.00-23.00hrs.

Facilities include a television room, library and boutique. Tennis, billiards and petanque are popular. Guests have one complimentary fishing-trip a week. Snorkelling gear is available.

Children are not permitted. Guests are mainly married couples. Accommodation here is sold within an all-inclusive, obligatory package.

Fishing

Denis has an established reputation for **fishing** off the Seychelles Bank, where the floor of the Indian Ocean plunges more than 6,500 feet (2,000m). It holds five world records for dog-tooth tuna. Twenty-three foot boats take a maximum of four persons in a party. Gear is provided although serious fishermen are advised to bring their own, especially artificial lures. On the way to the drop-off you are likely to see schools of bonito, mackerel and tuna. Huge manta rays are common. Trolling is mainly for tuna, kingfish, marlin, sailfish and dorado. Weigh-in facilities are available.

There is reasonable beachcasting in several places

There is wonderful swimming from the empty beaches of Denis island

on Denis – small grouper, coral trout, parrot fish and an odd, close-in jobfish give a good fight.

Bottom-fishing trips are made by arrangement. Lines and bait are provided with the open boat fishing on the coral plateau, a mile or two (1-3km) off shore. The chef will cook anything you may catch.

Warning: a considerable swell off the Seychelles Bank is likely to cause sea-sickness. Take precautions.

Getting There

Air Seychelles operates a daily charter service from Mahé to Île Denis – flight time 50 minutes.

DESROCHES
Amirantes Group
Desroches is a coral island lying 120 nautical miles (220km) southwest of Mahé. It is the main island in the Amirantes Group, (named 'Ilhas do Almirantes' by the Portuguese explorer Vasco da Gama when he passed that way). Three of the Amirantes islands – Desroches, D'Arros and Marie-Louise – have airstrips. Sea communications are maintained by the Islands Development Corporation, but you need clearance to land on the privately owned islands. Desroches was one of the main watersports centres in Seychelles until the island suffered severe damage in the republic's first-ever cyclone in 1990. The storm-damaged Desroches Island Lodge Hotel has been completely renovated, and the island is again open for business.

Desroches in the Amirantes group

Getting There

Desroches is linked to Mahé by Air Seychelles scheduled flights on Monday, Wednesday and Saturday – flight time one hour. Babies under two are taken free. There are excellent views of the island on landing.

Bookings should be made through:

Desroches-Island Resorts (Seychelles) Ltd, PO Box 638, Ocean Gate House, Victoria, Mahé (tel: 24502).

FRÉGATE

Inner Islands

A small botanical wilderness, Frégate, 35 miles (56km) east of Mahé, is the most isolated of the granitic group of islands surrounded by coral reefs. Like the other granite isles, Frégate was at one time frequented by pirates. A member of a natural history party which visited the island in 1933 wrote of seeing traces of pirate settlement... boxes filled with Spanish piastres... crockery from various countries... cannon-balls and rock carvings apparently chiselled at random. Bones were scattered around several coral tombs and elderly Seychellois spoke of finding gold *cruzados* on the beach. Among the first settlers to arrive on Frégate in 1802 was Louis Francis Serpholet, one of 70 Jacobin deportees to Mahé following an attempted assassination of Napoleon. Serpholet was shipped out to Frégate after rumours of a local plot to seize power. The first owner of Frégate, a member of the well-known Seychellois Savy family, raised a small herd of cattle brought from Madagascar. Acquired by German enterprise in 1962, Frégate is now run by a local manageress as a tourist attraction.

What to See

Nature is the main interest. The rare Seychelles magpie robin, whose melodious song earns it the local name of *Pie Chanteuse*, is the big attraction. Frégate is its last refuge. There are now 22 birds, quite tame, feeding on rice scattered around Plantation House (the island hotel).

Among other local birds are colonies of white, or fairy terns, the emblem of Air Seychelles. Invertebrates include a large centipede and a long-legged spider – be careful, both deliver a painful bite. Reptiles include the ubiquitous land tortoise and the usual skinks and lizards. There is no traffic. You can walk to any point on Frégate in 20 minutes. Popular walks go to Anse Victorin and Anse Parc, small settlements with beaches and fringed by lagoons.

Swimmers should beware of strong currents.

Accommodation

Plantation House, PO Box 459, Victoria, Mahé (tel: 23123). Built in 1975, the Plantation House has 10 basic rooms. Dress is casual. Children are permitted. A lunch-buffet is provided. Available only as an all-inclusive package.

Getting There

Frégate is a 15-minute flight from Mahé. Boat landings are difficult, so most people come to the island by air. Day trippers are welcome.

A day-excursion from Mahé is bookable at the Frégate Office on Revolution Avenue, Victoria, or via travel agents. The price includes air-fare, lunch and tour.

LA DIGUE

Inner Islands

Many visitors consider La Digue the nicest island in Seychelles. It certainly boasts the most spectacular coast in the inner, granitic group. Huge, wrinkled granite outcrops, blue lagoons and waving palms are a favourite 'fashion shoot'. *Robinson Crusoe* was filmed here.

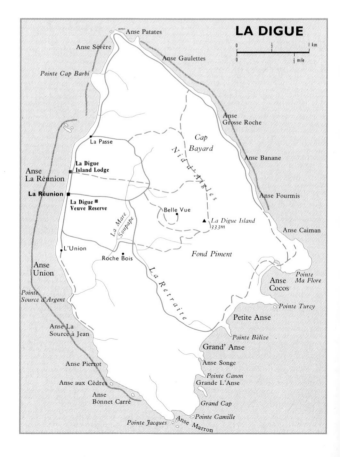

About 2,000 Seychellois live on La Digue, mainly fishermen and farmers of copra, vanilla, patchouli (which produces a fragrant oil) and vegetables. Some work in a small boat-building business; a copra factory employs others. The main community lives on the west coast between La Passe and La Réunion.

It is not only the beautiful scenery which endears La Digue to visitors but also the laid-back lifestyle. You sense it is somewhere special when the interisland schooner ties up at the pier at La Passe. There are no cars here – ox-cart taxis wait under the trees. Or you can rent a bicycle (see **Getting About** page 76).

La Digue is also a wonderful place for walks. The problem on a day-trip is seeing everything in the time. You really need two full days, one to complete the trail-walk, a second to visit the beaches. Advance room reservations are essential if you intend staying overnight.

What to See

The Seychelles Tourist Office's publication *Nature Trails and Walks in Seychelles – No 10 La Passe–Grand'Anse* is your best guide to sightseeing on La Digue.

◆◆◆
LA PASSE CIRCULAR WALK

La Passe on the west coast was founded by a score of political exiles from the island of Réunion, in 1798. Start the walk here and head south, towards the hospital. The spreading trees lining the road are mainly Indian almond and *takamaka*. *Takamaka* is likely to have once covered La Digue. Old boats and houses are made of its durable, hard red timber.

Follow the coastal road running parallel with Anse La Réunion. The island hospital is named after Sir Marston Logan, a British governor of Seychelles (1942-47). Further on are several traditional

La Passe, entry point to La Digue

plantation-style houses.
The branches of an avenue of trees touch overhead outside La Digue Island Lodge. The only tourist hotel, it is owned by local businessman Grégoire Payet who also owns the 'Grégoire Supermarket'.
On the same side there is a traditional coconut-crusher where oil is extracted by a press-bar harnessed to an ox walking round and round. This work was once done by two slaves. Beyond is a row of two-storey timber houses, La Digue school and St Mary's church. Beyond the end of the village is a large cross at a junction in the road. Not far away is the cemetery with graves of the early settlers from the island of Réunion (near Madagascar). If you walk straight ahead, you will pass the boat-building yard on your way to Grand'Anse. Take the left fork, across the central plateau. It is easy walking and cycling. On the right is the State Farm, on former swamp land. The vanilla plantation here is the biggest in Seychelles. Vanilla vines are like orchids and need the support of small trees. Plants by the roadside – wild poinsettia, star-of-Bethlehem and lantana – were all brought to La Digue by the early settlers. You will pass a farm, now in ruins, but covered in vivid white and purple bougainvillea.
A bridge spans an extensive marshland called 'Mare Soupape' after a freshwater terrapin, found only in wetlands on the granitic islands. Dragonflies dip over the marsh and frogs plop among the water-hyacinths. A pair of Chinese bitterns may be seen stalking tilapia (fish). Beyond the bridge, the central ridge of La Digue rises to a height of 1,092 feet (333m). There is a small store selling fruit, biscuits, soft drinks and beer.
The way is now dominated by fruit-trees. Among them are banana, breadfruit, mango and the Malay apple, or red *ponm*. Heading for the coast again, you pass another marshland area on your left. Further along is Bernique Guesthouse, on your right. The coastal road is reached in another five minutes' stroll.

◆◆◆
GRAND' ANSE WALK

Set off for Grand'Anse in the southeast of the island before it gets too hot. Once there you can swim – beware of strong currents at all times of the year – and relax under the shady trees. Take snacks and drinks as there are no shops.
From La Passe, follow the coastal track to the large concrete cross planted at a fork beyond St Mary's church (see also **La Passe Circular Walk**). Left goes to the farm and the marshes; you continue on through the coconut plantations. There is a small boat-building enterprise a few steps off the track on your right. Further on is a copra factory. Both can be seen. The trail now loops around a massive granite outcrop known as the *Citadelle*. The way between giant boulders

becomes too sandy for cyclists: if you have come by bike, it is safe left against a rock. Grand'Anse and Petit Anse are two of the world's most popular fashion shoots. Photographers fly thousands of miles for this backdrop. The bays are surrounded by spectacular granite outcrops like sculpture in a Henry Moore exhibition. The lagoon is shallow at low tide. You can snorkel on the reef. Take plastic shoes for walking on the coral. The walk back to the jetty at La Passe takes about 40 minutes.

◆◆
VEUVE RESERVE
The Seychelles black paradise flycatcher is unique to La Digue. It feeds on insects attracted to the island's wetlands. There is a special reserve for the birds near Bill's Bridge (named after William Dorian, an Englishman who lived on La Digue). A wooden board on the left, along the trail to Grand'Anse, indicates the reserve. Roads are unmarked, but once there you can always ask a local. For more on this beautiful bird see: **Peace and Quiet** page 89.

Accommodation
You really need to stay several days to appreciate La Digue, but at time of writing, the island had only one hotel and two guesthouses.
Bernique Guesthouse, La Réunion (tel: 34229). Quiet, five-room family residence run by a warm Diguois woman, 10 minutes' walk inland from La Digue Island Lodge and 30

At work in La Digue's copra factory

minutes' walk to Grand'Anse. Creole meals available on request. Cheap.
Choppy's Bungalows/Bar, Anse La Réunion (tel: 34224). Basic twin-bedded rooms. Near Anse La Réunion and 30 minutes' walk to Grand'Anse. Creole meals. Bar/dance-hall, lively on a Saturday night. Cheap.
La Digue Island Lodge, Anse La Réunion (tel: 34232). Smarter, tourist-style chalets under shady trees. All air-conditioned. Across the road, the 'Yellow House' has single and duplex-style (two-level) accommodation for a family and child. Bathroom has a bath as well as a shower. Children under two in parents' room free. Tropical-style bar and restaurant with tables on the

sand. Creole-tourist type menu, good wine list with six different champagnes. Swimming-pool. Bookings essential. Credit cards accepted. Moderate–expensive. Full board.

You can rent a cycle at La Passe

Restaurants
Apart from La Digue Island Lodge (see above), there is: **Patatran Restaurant**, Anse Patates (tel: 34353). In the far northeast of the island, it is 30 minutes' stroll from La Passe, or 15 minutes by ox-cart taxi. Good Creole-style meals, seafood a speciality. Attractive viewpoint. Licensed. Cheap.

Getting There
A daily schooner service operates between Mahé and La Digue, via Praslin. Actual sailing time is roughly three hours and from June to August it may be very rough indeed. The majority of visitors fly to Praslin to catch the ferry to La Digue. It is advisable to book

ahead during the peak tourist periods. You can do this direct with travel agents on Praslin, or via your hotel. The trip takes about 30 minutes.

Getting About
On La Digue, you walk, cycle or take an ox-cart. **Bicycles** may be rented from the rank on the pier at La Passe. Sand in places makes cycling difficult and your brakes are unlikely to work should a chicken cross the road. Fifteen **ox-cart taxis** operate on La Digue. The animals – Brahmin bulls – pull 10 people at walking pace. You can have a day's tour by ox-cart; price includes driver-guide and assistant.

Facilities
A post office with public call-box is found near the pier at La Passe.
'La Passe Store' sells postcards, soft drinks and

biscuits, as well as the array of polishes and detergents required by the houseproud Seychelloise.

There is a Barclays Bank (tel: 34348).

Medical treatment can be obtained at Logan Hospital (tel: 34255).

Excursion

Boat-trips can be made from La Digue to Félicité. A granitic island with lush vegetation, **Félicité** lies about two miles (3km) off the east coast of La Digue. Its dozen inhabitants are involved in fishing, farming and the copra industry. A chalet-style lodge overlooks a tranquil cove. There is good snorkelling. Bookings and further information from La Digue Island Lodge.

SILHOUETTE
Inner Islands

Silhouette is the misty blue island visible 12 miles (19km) off northwest Mahé. Although only 75 minutes away by boat, it remains one of the least known inner granitic islands in Seychelles. The main reason is the difficulty of disembarking passengers, a procedure almost as tricky as it was some 200 years ago when the first settlers arrived. You have to transfer from a larger boat to a small outboard and ride ashore through a pass in the reef. The manoeuvre is dangerous during a strong wind, or at low tide. Because of the uncertain landing the only hotel, Silhouette Island Lodge, cannot accept the responsibility of day-visitors.

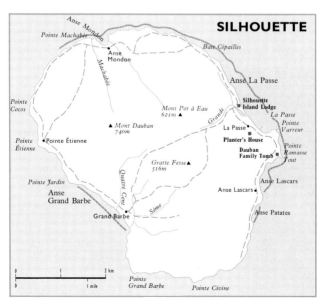

One or two visitors can probably manage, but there are obvious risks in trying to land a tour-group. For independent travellers, taking a breaker is part of the Silhouette adventure.

Silhouette is even quieter than La Digue. There are no ox-carts, not even a bicycle. The only wheelmarks are made by a tractor bringing goods off the schooner from Mahé which discharges 'on the roads'.

La Passe, the main settlement, has 150 residents who live in neat timber houses along the path leading from the jetty to the farm – the main road on Silhouette.

The community counts a hospital, school, church and shop. The shop opens on Wednesday and Friday from 08.00-15.00hrs. It stocks fish-hooks, Cheddar cheese, eggs, cloves, garlic, mosquito coils,

soap-powder, cigarettes and beer.

No money is used on Silhouette. People sign for purchases and the account is paid by the administrator. There is no bank and there are no credit card facilities, but the island is so uncommercialised you will not even find a postcard to buy.

Caught in a time-warp, Silhouette is probably the most interesting among the inner islands in Seychelles. Its main attraction for scientists as well as nature-lovers is the tangled forests, barely explored.

The shop may one day sell 'Sunstroke' T-shirts, but it is unlikely the island will ever be more commercialised, as granite outcrops rule out an airport, and behind the coastal clearing is a wilderness.

Supply ship off Silhouette's reef

History

The third largest island after Mahé and Praslin, Silhouette was discovered by Arab mariners, or *lascars*. Older Seychellois living at Anse Lascars recall Muslim graves where sailors had buried comrades drowned in a shipwreck. Several tombs had inscriptions in Arabic. All have since been washed away, or overgrown by the jungle. One of the first mentions of Silhouette is in the log of a voyage made by a British ship during a passage to India on 20 January 1609. The next record does not seem to be until 28 January 1771, a time when Hanoverian England was agog with the discovery of the great southern continent of Australia.

The French called the island Silhouette, after the politician Étienne de Silhouette (whose name was also given to 'silhouette' outline portraits). In common with other granitic islands in Seychelles, Silhouette probably witnessed the comings and goings of pirates. The colourful pirate Hodoul is thought to have used Silhouette as a stage for sorties, but according to Hodoul descendants on Mahé, he never lived there. The rough seas slapping the reefs meant that a pirate chased by naval vessels could not seek shelter quickly. Slipping out quietly at night was similarly impossible.

In the 19th century, Auguste Dauban, a French officer who had fought at Waterloo, began buying up parcels of land on Silhouette. It is said that the last plot was owned by an old African who agreed to sell on condition the sale included a violin. Legend claims it was a Stravidarius, but more probably it was an ordinary Madagascan fiddle which caught his eye when invited on board Dauban's boat.

The Daubans were hard-working proprietors. The old man planted vanilla, rubber, citronella and cloves, the latter still being harvested. His son, Henri, now in his nineties and living on Mahé, attended the London School of Economics and threw javelin at the 1924 Paris Olympics – a skill acquired spearing fish on Silhouette. This was a true Swiss Family Robinson. You can see the remarkable

Dauban mausoleum at Pointe Ramasse Tout, south of La Passe.

Silhouette remained in the Dauban family until 1983, when it passed to the Seychelles government. It is now run by Islands Development Corporation.

What to See

In addition to La Passe, there are two settlements on Silhouette – Grand Barbe and Anse Mondon – both of which can be reached on foot but are easier to visit by boat, although landing on the rocks is rough. Take shoes but wear your swimming costume in anticipation of a dunking.

◆
GRAND BARBE

You need a machete to hack your way across the island from La Passe to Grand Barbe on the west coast. The three-mile (5km) walk each way takes about a day there and back. Take something to drink. A guide is also advisable. Grand Barbe has about 30 inhabitants, scratching a living from farming and fishing.

◆
ANSE MONDON

The coastal route from La Passe to Anse Mondon on the northern side of Silhouette is also barred by foliage. Huge millipedes rustle in the leaves. At dusk fruit-bats fly down from Mont Dauban to feast on the mangoes. Only three families live here. By boat, the trip from La Passe takes 15 minutes.

♦♦♦
TO ANSE LASCARS

The walk from Silhouette Island Lodge through La Passe to Anse Lascars takes about 1½ hours. Done at leisure it takes a morning. Wear shorts and ordinary footwear, but take a costume for swimming at Anse Lascars (but be very careful of currents).

Cross the bridge over the lagoon. On your left is a nursery school built following a visit to Silhouette by President René. The island hospital, with a spectacular view of the lagoon, is also on your left. The large plantation-style house in La Passe was the former Dauban family residence.

The long jetty at the eastern end of the bay is a good fishing spot at high tide. Ask locally about bait. A letter-box by the jetty is emptied when the schooner arrives from Mahé.

Next door is the warehouse and around the corner, in a stone shed, the island blacksmith or knife-grinder. The coconut-crusher is further along on the right.

Now you reach one of several shallow lagoons on the coast of Silhouette. Stand still and watch the curious rock-hoppers or amphibious fish, hopping about in the mud.

A flock of pet guinea fowl guards the **Dauban family tomb** at Pointe Ramasse Tout, framed in tall coconut-palms. The most eccentric structure in Seychelles, it is cast as a replica of L'Eglise de la Madeleine, in Paris.

Continue walking uphill, where the lush jungle suddenly ends in granite cliffs. Resist the temptation to climb them. One slip on a moist patch of rock

The Dauban mausoleum on Silhouette

and you will fall down hundreds of feet. There is a good panorama of Anse Lascars from here: wreathed in clouds, Mahé is visible. Return to the hotel via the same route. A safe swimming spot is the small bay to the east of the jetty.

◆◆◆
MONT DAUBAN

Mont Dauban rises to a height of 2,428 feet (740m) in the centre of Silhouette. Relatively few visitors manage to reach its peak. It is a hot struggle up, with tangled bushes plucking at your clothes. Carry the minimum, but include water and a machete. To get to the top and back, set off from the hotel by 07.00hrs. With no problems, you should be back in time for tea.

Above 1,900 feet (600m) you will encounter the strange pitcher plant – 'Lyan potato' in Creole, *Nepenthes pervelli* in Latin. Its favourite habitat is the misty, high altitude forest of Silhouette. The small, softer plants with closed lids are the juveniles. Mature adult plants have an open lid and a cylinder containing sticky fluid. Insects which fall in are broken down by enzymes, but a unique Seychelles mosquito manages to breed inside the pitcher without the larvae falling victim to the plant's penchant for meat.
A highlight of local flora, pitchers are found in abundance on Mont Pot à Eau on the way from La Passe to Mont Dauban.
Keep your eyes open for

Granite cliffs are a landscape feature of Silhouette

orchids as you climb. Many are so tiny and uncommon they have no vernacular names. Rare trees include the *basquea (Tri Lepsium madagascariense)*, only discovered in 1983, high up on Mont Dauban. Up to 30-50 feet (10-15m) tall, the tree has soft wood which contains a high percentage of water; when cut, it releases a milky fluid which turns the colour of blood.
The *Heritiera littoraslis* is another exhibit in the exotic garden covering Silhouette. The explorer Brayer du Barre observed, in 1775, a specimen with 'roots large enough to obtain a table of 15 seats from a single, unbroken piece'. Its local name is *Bois de Table*.

See **Peace and Quiet** for further descriptions of Seychelles' primeval forests.

◆◆◆
FARM WALK
The round-trip from the Silhouette Island Lodge to the State Farm and back takes about a leisurely hour. Follow the track out of the hotel and along the beachfront. The farm can be visited if you notify the manager in advance. One.of the biggest in Seychelles, it grows a variety of vegetables and raises chickens and goats. Both eat debris from the coconut factory.

Walk around behind the farm until you reach a lagoon. Like other fresh water on Silhouette, it teems with fish. Barb grow to a pound (half a kilo), but many die when it becomes too hot. Large local mud-crabs are never short of food.

The church is simple, but greatly loved and always full to overflowing on Sunday. Note the house with a TV aerial planted ingeniously on a headless palm-tree. In 100 metres from here you rejoin the track from La Passe.

Accommodation
Silhouette Island Lodge, PO Box 608, Victoria, Mahé (tel: 24003). Guests at the island hotel stay in 12 spacious timber bungalows set back from the beach with comfortable beds, plenty of fresh air and wardrobe space. Bathrooms have separate WC.

There are two executive bungalows. Each has an extra bedroom and a refrigerator.

All bungalows have a veranda with a beautiful view of the lagoon. The hotel has a pleasant, open-air restaurant. A fixed three-course menu features Italian and Creole meals, mainly fish, pasta and banana-based sweets. There is no à la carte. A full English breakfast is served. The bar is casual, but well stocked. It serves excellent espresso coffee. Magazines, mainly Italian, and board-games are available, but take anything to Silhouette you are likely to need. Children are welcome and the hotel can arrange boating and fishing trips. A windsurfer is available for hire, but conditions are tricky. Note that Silhouette Island Lodge does not accept credit cards.

Getting There
Most holidays on Silhouette are booked in advance through Island Relais, or a tour operator. The hotel cruiser completes the voyage Mahé–Silhouette in 75-90 minutes depending on weather conditions. The return fare is very expensive. The Island Development Company schooner sails at least twice weekly to La Passe. Passengers disembark into a small outboard. The voyage by schooner can be extremely rough and takes at least three hours.

Departures from Marine Charter, Victoria (hotel cruiser) and Interisland Quay (schooner). Times vary. Check the night before and early on the day of scheduled sailing.

PEACE AND QUIET

Wildlife and Countryside in Seychelles

by Paul Sterry

Seychelles provides an ideal setting for the trip of a lifetime, and doubly so if the visitor has an interest in natural history. Exotic plants flourish and sea birds in profusion feed around the coast and breed on some of the more remote or protected islands.

In the distant past, the Seychelles were joined to the other land masses that now border the Indian Ocean in the super-continent known as Gondwanaland. As India, Madagascar, Australia and Africa drifted apart, so the Seychelles became isolated. Some of the islands' wildlife testifies to this ancient continental association: primitive amphibians and palms lived here before the land masses separated. Other plants and animals are more recent colonists. Many coastal plants probably reached the Seychelles having drifted across the sea as seeds, while most of the land birds have close relatives in Madagascar, Africa or India and are, therefore, only comparatively recent arrivals in geological terms.

Man has had the greatest impact of any of the new arrivals, altering the natural vegetation across much of the lowlands and introducing predators and competitors which have upset the natural balance and, in many cases, adversely affected the endemic species. Sadly, 13 of the endemic subspecies or species of birds are endangered, some of them now having total world populations of less than 100 individuals. Their survival is in the hands of the Seychelles authorities and world conservation organisations.

Lush forests clothe Mahé

PEACE AND QUIET

In and Around Victoria

Mahé is most people's initial stop-off point in Seychelles. Although much of the natural vegetation has long-since disappeared from around Victoria – mangrove swamps around the shore line having been removed and the lowland forests cleared – there is still wildlife to see in and around the city.

Much of the coastal belt is agricultural, and among the plantations a good range of birds can be found, although many of them are not native. Head out of Victoria in any direction and you are likely to encounter this habitat. Cattle egrets, which colonised Seychelles of their own accord, search for insects and frogs. Introduced species include Madagascar turtle doves and barred ground doves, which forage on the ground, Indian mynahs and the brightly coloured Madagascar fody.

Fodys

Fodys are sparrow-sized birds which feed on insects and seeds. Two species are found in Seychelles, the endemic Seychelles fody and the introduced Madagascar fody. The latter is now widespread and the two species coexist on the islands of Cousin, Cousine and Frégate. The male Madagascar fody is a colourful bird with bright red plumage, and it was for its attractive appearance that it was introduced.

Despite the predominance of introduced species, a few endemic birds can still be found in the lowlands. Cave swiftlets are often seen overhead. These birds are so-called because they nest in caves, cementing the structure to a rock face. They feed on the wing, catching insects as they swoop through the air. They are usually seen in small groups and their scythe-like silhouette in flight is distinctive. Seychelles sunbirds and Seychelles bulbuls are also reasonably common. Even the occasional Seychelles kestrel can be found, this species having suffered through competition for nest sites with barn owls. The owls were introduced in a vain attempt to control the islands' rodent population but instead found nesting fairy terns much easier targets.

Wildlife interest around Victoria is not restricted to birds by any means. The songs of cicadas are a constant feature of the evenings, and grasshoppers, crickets and praying mantids abound. Noisy communal roosts of Seychelles fruit bats, high up in tall trees, are a common sight, the animals taking to the wing at dusk to go in search of fruits such as cashew fruits, mangoes, jackfruits and breadfruits.

The **Botanical Gardens** near Victoria (see also page 24) are well worth visiting. In this delightful setting, visitors can see all six endemic palms, including the coco-de-mer, as well as hundreds of other plants from all around the world. As an added bonus, there is a good chance of finding three of the endemic bird species: Seychelles sunbird, Seychelles bulbul and Seychelles kestrel.

Around the Coasts

The coastline around the islands of the Seychelles is far from uniform: above the tideline there are sandy beaches, rocky shores and mangroves, while beneath the water, coral reefs and rich meadows of sea grass flourish in the clean environment of the Indian Ocean. Although the birdlife is prolific, other coastal and marine animals and plants more than repay inspection. In some places, shells collect on the strandline, but visitors should be warned that it is illegal to collect them: admire and take photographs but leave them behind for others to admire.

The mangroves which fringe some beaches are rich in invertebrate life. Oysters attach to the roots and marine snails find welcome shelter. However, it is the fiddler crabs – males have one of their pincers brightly coloured and highly enlarged – that are most endearing as they scurry across the surface of the mud, never straying too far from their burrows. The area around Port Glaud is a particularly good example of mangrove.

Snorkelling

To see the offshore world at its best, you need to go snorkelling or at least to use a

A red headed fody

face mask. Close inshore, areas of sea grass can be found and these harbour large numbers of fish, molluscs (including cone shells and cowries) and strange marine creatures such as sea cucumbers. These sea grass beds are also feeding grounds for green turtles and young hawksbill turtles – adult hawksbills feed on coral – and these superbly adapted marine reptiles are sometimes seen in the marine parks. Seychellois fishermen were formerly permitted to catch a limited number of turtles for personal consumption, but a government ban on the practice was introduced following abuse of the permit system.

Snorkelling really comes into its own on the edge of coral reefs. Here you will find sea urchins – many have sharp spines so swim in plimsolls – cushion stars, brittlestars and much more. It is the fish, however, that are the stars of the coral reefs; where they are protected in the marine parks, they sometimes become extremely tame and inquisitive. Visit **Sainte Anne Marine National Park** (see also page 39) to the east of Victoria for excellent snorkelling; glass-bottomed boats ferry visitors from Victoria Harbour. Port Launay Marine National Park off Mahé's west coast also has outstanding marine life as does Anse Royale Bay in southwest Mahé.

Even without their associated inhabitants, **coral reefs** are fascinating habitats: despite their rock-like appearance they are living structures, built by millions of tiny, colonial animals. Each creature builds a calcareous skeleton for protection and, although they have stinging tentacles to catch minute particles in the water, they also have algae within their cells. These photosynthesise – energy from the sun is used to make food – so corals will only thrive in relatively shallow water where sunlight can penetrate and where there is enough food in the water for them to eat but not enough silt to clog them. Corals come in all shapes and sizes; in the seas around the Seychelles visitors can find sea fans, staghorn corals, flat, plate-like corals, and domed and jagged-edged colonies.

Forest Life of Seychelles

Although, at first glance, most of Seychelles is lush and green, much of the original vegetation has been destroyed or altered by man. This is especially true of the coastal lowlands, where plantations and small-scale farming have largely replaced the forests. However, by ascending the hills and mountains, particularly on Mahé and Silhouette, areas of upland forest can still be found. The

Skunk clown fish, a reef dweller

Birds of the Coast
Although truly oceanic sea birds, such as terns, frigatebirds and tropicbirds, can be seen almost anywhere from the coast, there is an interesting range of coastal birds that can be found on the shore itself. Some of these, such as cattle egrets and green herons, are resident birds, but the greatest variety can be found in migrant waders which arrive in September and October, having flown south to escape winter in the northern hemisphere. Intertidal mudflats – even those close to Victoria – provide rich feeding grounds for species such as greenshanks, grey plovers, greater sandplovers, curlew sandpipers and whimbrels. The latter species is sometimes also found on rocky shores in the company of turnstones and is easily told by its long, downcurved beak and black and white crown stripes.

Morne Seychellois National Park protects the best example of this habitat on Mahé and also harbours two of Seychelles' most endangered endemic birds.
The forests that once covered the coastal lowlands would have been distinctly different in character from the highland forests. Trees, such as *capucin, bois de fer* and *bois rouge*, would have reached great sizes but now only scattered specimens are found.

Away from the coast, some of the higher wooded habitats are classified as dry forest and, not surprisingly, they have suffered more than most from fire damage. The best remaining unspoilt area of natural dry forest is in the Vallée de Mai on Praslin, which is also the only remaining site for wild coco-de-mer palm and Seychelles black parrots.
Some of the upland areas reach sufficient altitude to create their own microclimate: often shrouded in mist and cloud, the forests are damp and lush. Fortunately, the best remaining areas lie within the protection of the **Morne Seychellois National Park**, while there are still tracts of unspoilt mist forest on **Silhouette**.
At intermediate altitudes, the forests, comprising species such as *bois merle, bois de montagne* and *bois maret*, as well as *capucin* and *bois rouge*, are lush. Epiphytic plants – species which do not root in the ground but instead are attached to trees – including begonias, ferns and orchids, are common, insect life abounds and caecilians – legless, worm-like amphibians – crawl through the leaf litter. Birds to look for in the hill forests include Seychelles sunbird, Seychelles bulbul and Seychelles blue pigeon. Visitors will be extremely fortunate if they see either a Seychelles grey white-eye or a Seychelles bare-legged Scop's owl, even though almost all their range lies within the

PEACE AND QUIET

The extraordinary pitcher plant

Morne Seychellois National Park. Both thought to be extinct until rediscovered in 1962 and 1959 respectively, they are indeed 'blue-riband' birds when it comes to Seychelles birdwatching.

Above about 1,500 feet (460m), the forest becomes stunted and more open. In patches of peaty, moist soil, visitors may find one of the most extraordinary plants on the Seychelles – the pitcher plant – which has developed a bizarre means of supplementing its intake of nutrients. It is a climbing plant, and it sometimes festoons the lower branches of trees with leaves which have become modified to form flasks. When mature, a lid, which covers the flask, opens to reveal a strong-smelling liquid which insects find irresistible. But the inner surface of the pitcher provides little grip and so the victim falls into the liquid trap, its nutrients to be digested by the plant. Try the Trois Frères Nature Trail for a forest walk. The car park and start of the walk are on the road south from Victoria to Sans Souci just past the Forestry Division offices. The trail continues to Dans Cèdres.

Praslin and the Vallée de Mai National Park

Praslin is most famous for the Vallée de Mai National Park. Here visitors can see the finest mixed palm forest in the whole of Seychelles, and this is the best site for the renowned endemic palm, coco-de-mer. The **coco-de-mer** is an extraordinary plant. Few visitors fail to be intrigued either by its appearance or by facts and figures about its biology. The leaves are enormous and the nuts, which resemble a female human pelvis, are the largest seeds in the plant kingdom, often weighing over 30 pounds (14kg). It takes two years for them to germinate and, having done so, it is then another 25 years before the trees can bear fruit. Each tree produces flowers of only one sex and it takes seven years for the fruit to mature after the female flower is successfully pollinated. The name 'coco-de-mer' reflects some of the mystery that formerly surrounded the palm's origins prior to its discovery in Seychelles. Although the seeds are not especially buoyant in saltwater, they were occasionally carried by currents to far-away shores in the Indian Ocean. The source of these strange nuts was unknown and was thought to be a huge submarine plant, hence the name.

The Vallée de Mai is also home to the rare **Seychelles black parrot**, an endemic subspecies, of which perhaps only 100-200 are left. A rather elusive bird, the black parrot spends much of its time high in the trees, feeding on fruits. Its high-pitched call – frequently imitated by Indian mynahs – sometimes gives a clue as to its whereabouts. The birds nest in holes in decaying coco-de-mer palms and screwpines. Also see pages 56–7.

La Digue

The delightful island of La Digue harbours Seychelles' smallest nature reserve and one of the islands' most elegant and endangered endemic birds. The **Seychelles black paradise flycatcher**, called locally 'veuve' – literally meaning 'widow', after the long black tail-streamers of the male – is comparatively easy to see and is one of La Digue's important tourist attractions. The female is quite different from the male, having a black head, chestnut back and tail and white underparts, and lacks the long tail-streamers.

Once widespread on other Seychelles islands, the paradise flycatcher is now more or less restricted to La Digue, where patches of lowland forest, comprising *takamaka* and *badamier* trees still remain. Its nest, which is a beautiful construction held together with silk from spiders' webs, is built among the branches of these trees, often surprisingly close to houses and tracks. An important feature of the reserve is the wetland area where insects thrive and serve as food for the flycatchers; this is where the birds feed and are most easily seen.

The Veuve Reserve is open Monday to Saturday from 09.30 until 12.00 and from 14.00 to 16.30hrs. The entrance is alongside the central road. Also see page 75.

Frégate

Frégate has the last remaining population of the **Seychelles magpie robin**. There are only about 11 breeding pairs left in the world, and so this species is teetering on the edge of extinction.

Magpie robins are extremely tame, sometimes feeding at the feet of visitors or even in houses. Sadly, their trustful nature caused their downfall: once common and widespread on most of the islands, they were vulnerable to introduced animals: cats caught them on the ground and their nests were sometimes destroyed by rats. Indeed, cats almost caused their extinction on Frégate, but fortunately these alien predators were eradicated.

The coastal fringe of Frégate, home to the magpie robins,

PEACE AND QUIET

was once covered in natural woodland. This has almost completely gone, having been replaced by small-scale agriculture. Fortunately, the magpie robins have adapted to this new environment well, feeding in the cultivated fields and nesting in coconut palms. Visitors to Frégate should also look for common noddys, the Seychelles fody – another highly endangered endemic species – and its more colourful relative, the introduced Madagascar fody.

Cousin

The delightful, granitic island of Cousin is a nature reserve where sea birds breed in huge numbers. Until recently, it was the last refuge for the **Seychelles brush warbler** and it harbours huge populations of two endemic species of skinks which feed on scraps of food, dead chicks, eggs and droppings from the sea bird colonies.

In 1968, the International Council for Bird Preservation bought Cousin, primarily in an attempt to halt the decline of the Seychelles brush warbler and prevent its imminent extinction – numbers had dropped to around 40 birds. The replacement of its natural habitat – native woodland – with coconut plantations had driven the birds to live in small patches of mangrove. However, by allowing native trees to grow among the coconuts, and thus creating semi-natural woodland, the warbler's numbers are recovering dramatically.

Most visitors to Cousin will be struck, not by the warblers, but by the breeding sea birds: over 200,000 pairs breed on the island, more than half of which are lesser noddys. Fairy terns, which lay their single egg precariously on branches, mainly in December, are common, and white-tailed tropicbirds also boast around 1,000 pairs. Wedge-tailed shearwaters, which nest in underground burrows, are nocturnal visitors to their breeding colonies, and non-breeding visitors include crested terns, frigatebirds and the occasional red-tailed tropicbird.

Cousin also has a healthy population of the endemic Seychelles fody. Although its introduced relative, the Madagascar fody, is also present, the native bird predominates. It is thought that the greater incidence of natural vegetation – and hence native insects and nectar – may explain the endemic species' success compared with Cousine and Frégate where both birds also occur. The presence of so many sea birds allows the fodys to scavenge food scraps and droppings around the colonies. Also see pages 64–7.

Bird Island

Bird Island (or Île aux Vaches) provides visitors with one of the greatest wildlife spectacles in the world: hundreds of thousands of sea birds – mainly sooty terns – breed in dense colonies and their comparative indifference to human presence allows wonderful views to be had. Some 600,000-800,000 pairs of sooty terns nest here, with most nesting starting in June. Over the years, the nesting colony has expanded as coconut plantations have been cleared to create open ground. Each bird nests a discreet distance from its neighbour – usually just beyond beak stabbing range – and the sight, sound and smell of the colony is unforgettable. In addition to the sooty terns, Bird Island also has a few pairs of superficially similar bridled terns nesting there, and about 10,000 pairs of common noddys, which breed in the coconut plantations and casuarina trees. Several hundred fairy terns are also present, and frigatebirds and tropicbirds can be seen offshore.

Also see pages 62–3.

Aride

Despite the implication of its name, Aride, the most northerly of the granitic islands, is lush and verdant. Like Cousin, it too has vast numbers of breeding sea birds, but here it is the lesser noddy that is most numerous. The lesser noddy is a species of tern which habitually nests in trees, and every available site seems to be occupied. Over 150,000 pairs regularly breed here, making Aride of worldwide importance for this species. They are attractive birds with dark brown plumage and a pale greyish head. The bill is long and fine and the tail looks long in flight. They feed far out to sea, picking small fish off the surface of the water. Their English name refers to their habit of nodding and bowing to

Nesting noddys on Cousin

PEACE AND QUIET

Great frigatebird in mating display

world. The world's largest coral atoll, the island has fabulous coral reefs and harbours a truly unique collection of plants and animals. All in all, it entirely justifies its designation as a World Heritage Site.

The immense central lagoon which dominates Aldabra was created by erosion rather than by coral formation. The island has the original population of giant tortoises and provides some excellent and undisturbed beaches for nesting green turtles. Sea birds nest in abundance among the mangroves, with lesser frigatebirds, great frigatebirds and red-footed boobies being among the highlights.

Aldabra is home to several endemic birds found nowhere else in the world. Sadly, the Aldabra brush warbler has probably become extinct in the last few years, but Aldabra sacred ibises, Aldabra fodys and white-throated rails – endemic subspecies – and Aldabra drongos are still holding on. The rails on Aldabra are flightless, an adaptation to life on remote islands with no ground predators, once common to many islands in the Indian Ocean. Inevitably, with the discovery of these islands came the arrival of man's travelling companions – rats and cats – with the consequent demise of these vulnerable birds. The rails on Aldabra are the only surviving species of flightless rails left anywhere in the whole Indian Ocean region.

each other while courting. Roseate terns and red-tailed tropicbirds breed on Aride in small numbers and great frigatebirds, although non-breeders, are often present and can be seen chasing other sea birds in an attempt to force them to disgorge their last meal. Frigatebirds are superbly adapted to life at sea. They never rest on the water – their feathers would become waterlogged – relying instead on their flying skill to intercept other sea birds and pick scraps of food from the water's surface. If the bones and feathers of a frigatebird were to be weighed separately, the feathers would weigh more than the bones: a true adaptation to life on the wing. Also see page 61.

Aldabra

Anyone fortunate enough to get to the far-flung island of Aldabra, will be visiting one of the most remote spots in the

FOOD AND DRINK

Seychellois cooking can be described as exotic, eclectic and limited. Traditional dishes are based on fresh seafood with pungent spices – especially pepper, ginger and chilli. Root vegetables such as yams, cassava and sweet potato are popular, while coconut is widely used in delicious curries and desserts. Unfortunately you are only likely to encounter true Seychellois cooking in a private home, so jump at an invitation. Many restaurants feature curious hybrid dishes, believing they appeal to tourist taste (crab in the shell with pasta is an Italian-Creole hybrid).

Local cooking draws on many cuisines – African, French, English, Indian, Chinese, Malay – with a penchant for sauces exceeding even that of France. Tasty Indian Ocean fish does not need a sauce, but getting a plain, grilled tuna steak is not easy.

Breadfruit is always found in some form on a local table. Weighing up to 4½ pounds (2kg) and grown throughout the year, it is the staff of life. According to an old saying, anyone who partakes of its fruit is guaranteed to return to Seychelles.

An order for chips may produce not potato, but the drier, more floury fingers of breadfruit. High in carbohydrate, it is used in casseroles or fried. Breadfruit (or *friyapen* in Creole) is also ground into flour.

Tropical fruits are the base of many local desserts. And what would the Seychellois do without the coconut? Coconut juice, often served in the nut, is a refreshing drink. Some visitors prefer it with the addition of sugar, or syrup. Grated coconut pulp is a delicious, creamy ingredient in main courses and many desserts. Biscuits, cakes and caramelised nougat are also made from coconut. Chopped coconut pieces are a chewy, in-between-meals snack.

Seafood

Not surprising in an island nation, seafood is king. But although the surrounding sea is home to scores of edible species, the same fish can appear with monotonous regularity.

Popular local eating fish are job, *caranque*, kingfish, dorado, *cordonnier*, *vielle*, *bourgeois* or red emperor, *rouget* and mackerel. Marlin and tuna are marketed through the Seychelles Marketing Board.

Keen fish-eaters should not miss savoury tuna fillets, baked *bourgeois* and sailfish fricassee. Home-smoked sailfish is a speciality in some places – go for it! Popular dishes are *kat-kat de banane* made from *caranque*, or tuna, coconut milk and plantain bananas. *Maquereau Boucaner* – mackerel steamed in banana leaves – is another favourite, though rather bland, dish.

Creole **fish-curries** are anything but bland if the chef

FOOD AND DRINK

has been too liberal with the spices. Some of the best feature bonito, mackerel or *caranque* cooked in creamy coconut milk. Curried octopus, or a combination of prawn and octopus, is delicious. Squid, or octopus salad, freshly baked *baguettes* and a crisp glass of *rosé* wine makes a delightful, light lunch.

Stuffed mussels and baby clams are found on most good menus. Baby shellfish are the basis of traditional *tec-tec* soup eaten with relish by the Seychellois and an excellent starter if well made.

Other Savoury Specialities

Tec-tec heads a short list of truly ethnic dishes, worth trying if you are adventurous. Hard-boiled, well-peppered **terns' eggs** are an appetiser for gourmets. The tern lays twice and the second egg is collected, quite legally; the eggs are sold in Victoria Market. The yolk is rich yellow and the taste is not fishy as you might imagine.

Another appetiser is **'millionaire's salad'** made from shredded heart of the coconut palm. Expensive, as the entire tree must be sacrificed, it has a soft texture with a delicate flavour. Do not allow the chef to smother it with strong French dressing.

Turtle is to the Seychellois what roast beef is to the British. It is said that a true Seychellois must have at least two turtle meat steaks a year, or he feels deprived. Visitors should, however, bear in mind the threatened state of some

species of turtle when ordering their meal.

Another unusual meat is flying fox (fruit bat). **Curried flying-fox** or **fruit bat braised in red wine** may be too *outré* for you but they are traditional dishes on Silhouette and Praslin. The bats are trapped in nets laid in the mango trees; their wing-span may reach a metre across but there is not a lot of meat on them.

Other meats have more recently taken over as bases of curries and fricassees. **Roast pork glazed with wild bee honey** is a gourmet dish for special occasions. A common dish is chicken and coconut curry, a rich, sometimes unctuous, dish, eaten with a side serving of Creole rice. Rice is a popular accompaniment to most main courses. *Riz Creole* is savoury rice mixed with onion, ginger, garlic and, occasionally, vegetables.

Fruits

Most of the fruits from the Garden of Eden must grow in Seychelles. Many visitors will be familiar with mango, pineapple and passionfruit, all sold in supermarkets in the West. Victoria Market is the best spot to identify other varieties. Most local fruits are seasonal, but some, like breadfruit, grow all through the year.

Popular local fruits to look for are:

Corasol: rough, green oval fruit with a spongy texture; makes an excellent sorbet – season December-February.

Jamalac: smooth-skinned, pinkish-white, cone-shaped fruit; apple-type texture, greatly loved by local tortoises – season June-August.

Jackfruit: huge, knobbly, green fruit with a soft, yellow flesh tasting of mixed fruits – season January-May and August-September.

Papaya: smooth-skinned, orange-green fruit with soft blandly-sweet flesh; best spiked with a squeeze of lime – grows all year.

Zat: or custard-apple, knobbly, round, pale-green fruit; tangy flesh surrounds black seeds – season December-February.

Fruit-based Desserts

Fried bananas and coconut cream are a heavenly end to dinner. The islands grow more than 20 different varieties of bananas. They range from tiny *mignons* to huge, red plantains. The mango rivals the banana as the queen of local fruit. Fourteen different types of mango flourish in the

Creole buffet on Denis. Job fish, centre, and pumpkin salad, right

equatorial climate, the season – October-January – being eagerly awaited by flying-foxes.

Fresh fruit salad dusted with cinnamon is a common dessert. Hotel buffets usually feature a chopped seasonal fruit dessert.

Preserves

Local fruits are also made into delicious chutneys and jams – papaya, passionfruit, guava, and lime and orange marmalade. Jams and local fruit chutneys are sold in Victoria Market and make novel gifts for friends.

Local Beverages

Fresh fruit juices are the main thirst-quenchers in Seychelles. Fresh lime-juice and soda goes down well. Other beverages are made from mango, passionfruit, pineapple and guava. The ubiquitous 'Welcome Drink' is usually a sickly, watered-down, mixed fruit cocktail. Simple coconut juice is best drunk neat. Coconut milk is the base of many cocktails. Hotels in the

FOOD AND DRINK/SHOPPING

Seychelles Hotels group serve some of the best: Banana Royale (coconut milk, pineapple juice, brown rum, ripe banana and cream) and Reef Sunrise (whisky, Tia Maria, brandy and coconut juice served in a whole coconut) are two to try.

'Toddy' or *calou* is a slightly *pétillant* palm-wine, whose pungent aroma settles after a glass or two. A pleasant tipple, it is best drunk about two to three days old (after six months' fermentation it turns to vinegar). Other fermented fruit juices will also get you going. *Bacca* made from fermented pineapple resembles rum – two or three *baccas* pack a kick like a mule.

The older generation of Seychellois still drink 'toddy', but young men prefer local 'Seybrew'. Brewed near Victoria, this light, pale ale enjoys huge sales.

An interesting anomaly in an avowedly socialist state is the number of excellent South African wines available. French wines and champagnes are also sold at a price.

There is no shortage of local tea in Seychelles, but any true tea-lover would sell his or her soul for a decent pot. Most hotels make tea with bags; if you like strong tea and ask for two bags, you will often pay double the price. Camomile tea is popular.

Coffee is generally awful. The Marie-Antoinette restaurant in Victoria (see page 49) makes a pleasant brew, spiked with vanilla. The Scala Restaurant at Bel Ombre on Mahé (see page

Coconut cocktail

49) and Silhouette Island Lodge (see page 82) serve Italian espresso coffee.

Do not drink the tap water on Mahé. 'Val Riche' is a good local mineral water from springs on Morne Seychellois.

SHOPPING

Mahé is the arts, crafts and curio centre of Seychelles. Victoria and 'Le Village Artisanal' (see page 35) near the Reef Hotel are the main shopping centres. Elsewhere shopping is limited to hotel boutiques and family-run curio businesses.

Praslin has around half a dozen souvenir shops selling T-shirts, postcards and curios.

Shopping on the other islands is very limited: you cannot even buy a postcard on Silhouette.

Specialities
Tea, Spice and All Things Nice

The Western trend for using spices has made prices shoot up, but locally grown cloves, vanilla, ginger and pepper remain good bargains. In Victoria Market, the centre stall, **JA Adriene**, sells everything for the cook. Take home some pure clove or vanilla essence. The mango and palm-heart chutney is probably made by Mr Adriene's wife. Local floral essences make good gifts – see **Kreolfleurage** (page 34). Teas can be bought at the **Tea Tavern** (see page 37). Teas, spices, etchings, shell objects and coco-de-mer are sold in the small duty-free shop at Mahé International Airport.

Woven Crafts

Many hand-woven articles are sold in Victoria. Bags and table-mats are popular, but visitors find a Seychellois hat is irresistible. Whether it looks as good on you as on a local fisherman is debatable, but a hat is essential to shade your face from the equatorial sun. The most stylish *chapeau de pêcheur* is made from finely woven palm-fronds. You can buy one of these hats in Victoria Market for the price of tea for two in London, or two and a child in New York; but the one that caught your eye on a Seychellois is always impossible to find.

Batik is something else to look out for.

For other information on what to buy, see **Mahé** page 50.

Don't Buys

It takes resistance not to buy turtle-shell as the range of earrings, picture frames, jewellery-boxes and spectacles is endless, and such items are among the most beautiful locally made objects. Do not give in. All are made from the shells of hawksbill or loggerhead turtles which are threatened with extinction and enjoy protection under the Washington Convention banning trade in endangered species.

Traders say their items come from stock-piles acquired before the ban, but stick to your principles and **don't buy**. The import of turtle-shell is prohibited by most countries and, as well as risking a fine, you are contributing to the demise of a creature who swam in the oceans before the days of the dinosaurs.

Other items to shun are shark jaws and walking sticks made from sharks' backbones. Tourist demand for such souvenirs has put every one of these great fish on a hit-list. Ignore too the tempting displays of shells. The Seychelles government may pass admirable conservation laws, but implementing them is another matter.

Art Galleries

There could be no more evocative souvenir than an authentic Seychelles picture. For details of artists and their work, see under **Culture** page 100.

It is easy to buy on impulse in a holiday environment, but you should ask yourself whether a jungle painting will look right at home.

If you have transport, go back several times to the painting

that captured your interest. An Adams silk-screen print sells for as little as SR300. The asking price of a Devoud original is SR3,000-7,000.
Gerard Devoud Gallery, PO Box 72, Victoria (tel: 47280). Situated at La Mamelles-old airport road, 2 miles (3km) from Victoria.
Open, every day 08.00-20.00hrs.
Michael Adams Gallery, PO Box 405, Victoria (tel: 71106). Studio at Anse aux Poules Bleues.
Open, weekdays 08.00-17.00hrs.
Atelier d'Art, State House Avenue, Victoria and **Christy's Gallery** in Quincy Street, Victoria have exhibitions of local artists.

ACCOMMODATION

Hotels and guesthouses are strictly controlled by the Seychelles government. They must belong either to the 'Seychelles Hoteliers Association' or the 'Small Hotels and Guesthouses Association', and standards are regulated by the Seychelles Tourist Office which issues licences.
The result of this is that, although standards of accommodation, service and facilities are dependably high, there are no cheap rooms to be had. Private accommodation does exist, but it is illegal to let a room without a licence. There is no problem finding a room except during holiday times – Christmas, New Year and Easter – when

hotels tend to be fully booked. Accommodation (of which about 65 per cent is on Mahé) ranges from tourist-style hotels with 100-200 rooms to small guesthouses with perhaps only three or four rooms. There are a few self-catering complexes on Mahé (see **Mahé Accommodation** page 47). Camping and sleeping rough on the beach are not allowed. First class hotels are, as you would expect, expensive. Tourist-style luxury hotels have variable rates according to the season, as follows:
Low: 22 April–29 July and 26 August–23 December
High: 9 January–21 April and 30 July–25 August
Peak: 24 December–8 January
Room prices in small hotels and guesthouses are fixed throughout the year. Middle range establishments charge on the higher side of low, but they offer some of the best accommodation in the Indian Ocean. Guesthouses offer good value. Enquire about special weekly rates.

Choosing a Hotel
Most visitors come to Seychelles on a package deal. Choosing a hotel from the tour operator's glossy brochure requires some reading between the lines. A few pointers might be helpful.

Type
Bungalow-style is best in the tropics. Nothing beats a thatch-roofed chalet on the beach (though this type of hotel is rare on Mahé). In block-style hotels you may be disturbed by anything from honeymooners

next door to the nightclub downstairs, while barking dogs, the family and TV can be a nuisance in a guesthouse.

Location

Mahé in particular has some charming, medium-size hotels, but you must choose the location carefully. While some are gorgeous, they may not have a swimming-beach. Others central to watersports are likely to be packed with tourists. If you choose a remote guesthouse location you will need to rent a car.

Service

Seychelles wins top marks for cleanliness. You are likely to be woken by the maid sweeping outside your window, or the gardener raking fallen frangipani. Reception and bar service ranges from superlative to downright surly – but remember the tourist industry is only two decades old.

CULTURE, ENTERTAINMENT AND NIGHTLIFE

Music and Dance

The Seychellois adore music and dancing. In a short time they have evolved their own forms of ethnic music and dance which have emerged from the mixed cultural heritage of the people.
The lively *camtole* has developed from the waltzes, polkas and quadrilles of the early French settlers, dances which are traditionally accompanied by violin, banjo, bass drum and triangle.

Seychelles' own dance – the séga

Likewise, the *contredanse* is of French origin – indeed, it is thought to go back to the dances of the court of Louis XIV. The *contredanse* is something like a square dance or a Scottish reel in that the dancers form figures.
While the *contredanse* is ever popular, the heart of most Seychellois lies in dances like the *moutia* and the *séga*, which have their origins in the rhythms of Africa. The *moutia* was a dance-song of the African slaves, originally sung and danced in a group around a fire out in the open, well away from the slaves' European masters. It still largely retains its exclusivity and mystery. The dance is characterised by erotic movements, though the male and female performers avoid physical contact. If anything, it resembles an Indian Ocean version of the Tahitian *tamure*, where the dancers' bodies

CULTURE, ENTERTAINMENT AND NIGHTLIFE

remain still above the waist. The *séga* shares the *moutia's* African origins. It is, however, a much more recent phenomenon, having grown up only over the past 15 or 20 years. It is perhaps the nearest thing to a Seychellois 'pop' music. Not a month passes without a new *séga* hit catching on in Mahé discos. Songs have a quick, catchy rhythm and are danced with great precision by couples. Traditional musical background to both dances is provided by the *zez*, a sort of monochord sitar and a perky one-string violin known as a *bow*. The rhythm for a genuine *séga* may be hammered out on a hollow coconut-palm. If you have the chance, do not miss either a *camtole* show or a *séga* cabaret. An authentic *moutia* is usually danced only at private parties, or on Liberation Day when people are enjoying themselves. However, some hotels put on a version of it as entertainment.

Art

Today Seychelles counts a score of artists developing personal themes, but painting is associated with the exuberant tropical school popularised by British artist Michael Adams.

The son of a rubber-planter in Malaya, Adams has lived for 20 years near Anse aux Poules Bleues in southwest Mahé. His bright watercolours shiver with life. You can smell his flowers and hear his insects, while lean figures carrying strings of fish almost walk out of the frame.

Gerard Devoud also uses vibrant aquarelles – green from the Vallée de Mai on Praslin and turquoise from the surrounding sea characterise his work.

Marc Duc, who worked with Adams between 1975 and 1978, initially drew inspiration from the Baie Lazare on Mahé's southwest coast, where

Typical painting by Gerard Devoud

he was born. After studies in France, his style has become pure expressionist. Leon Radegonde from La Digue executes everything from murals to Pop Art. Pacquerette Lableche is an equally well regarded expressionist. Born in 1951, Christine Harter is a traditional water-colourist painting on Praslin.

Entertainment

Several hotels on Mahé – Auberge Club des Seychelles, Beau-Vallon Bay, Coral Strand, Equator, Plantation Club, Le Meridien Barbarons and Le Meridien Fisherman's Cove, Northolme and Reef – offer local 'folk' dancing and singing as entertainment. On Praslin, similar entertainment can be enjoyed at the hotels L'Archipel, Flying Dutchman and Paradise.

Nightlife

While local nightlife is limited, there are several lively spots on Mahé, especially on Friday and Saturday evenings (see page 47). Praslin has a certain amount of nightlife (see page 60), but on the other islands the motto is 'early to bed and early to rise'. Videos have a big local following.

WEATHER AND WHEN TO GO

Lying approximately four degrees south of the equator, Seychelles experiences perpetual summer weather with the annual temperature averaging between 24° and 30°C (75°–86°F).

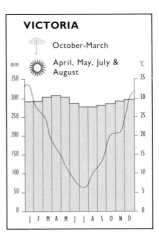

Winds

There are two different windy seasons: the southeast trade winds from May to October and the northwest monsoon from November to April. During the southeast trades humidity is low and rainfall should be minimal. However, in May 1990, Seychelles experienced torrential rains and the first cyclone on record, which devastated the island of Desroches. Wind is generally unlikely to exceed force 4-5, but seas can be very rough. During this period the outer islands experience near-perfect weather.

During the northwest monsoon the seas are calm and the wind is lighter. This is the hot season, and humidity is high, with a correspondingly heavy rainfall around Christmas. The climate and rainfall pattern (20-60 inches/500-1,500mm on the coral islands, reaching 140 inches/3,500mm on Morne Seychellois) promotes the luxuriant growth of vegetation characteristic of the granitic islands, in particular Silhouette.

When to Go

So what is the best time to go to Seychelles? Assuming you want to avoid the busiest times you could choose June and take a good supply of seasickness pills. Although humid, late October-November is also good. Be aware that Mahé – with Silhouette – is the wettest of the islands, and January is the wettest month. The best weather conditions are likely to be on one of the coral islands, such as Île Denis. If you are planning to stay in one of the more popular areas, note that Beau Vallon Bay on Mahé and Côte d'Or on Praslin are good during the southeast trades and Grand'Anse on Praslin is good during the northwest monsoon.

What to Wear

Unless you want to compete in low-key fashion stakes, you need next to nothing for a holiday in Seychelles. Take advantage of the casual attitudes to dress and pack for the tropical climate. Shorts and T-shirts are the order of the day, but keep your swimming costume for the beach. The Seychelloise may be liberated but she would not be seen on the road in a bathing-suit. Be a little more formal in Victoria. For trips, take jeans, a lightweight, waterproof jacket, a scarf for the wind, gym-boots, sandals and your beach-towel. You can buy a local hat

and sarong, or wrap-around, in Victoria Market.

If you stay at a smart hotel such as Sunset Beach, or L'Archipel on Praslin, you might feel more comfortable if you dress for dinner. But the vogue remains casual-chic. An essential item for inter-island hopping is a small back-pack. A 5-kilo load-all is ideal; choose one which can fit inside your case when not required. All hotels have left luggage facilities.

HOW TO BE A LOCAL

Only 250 years old, Seychellois society has not had time to develop a complex background of traditions and customs. Nevertheless, the ethnic mixture that forms the population – European, African and Asian – has produced a specifically Seychellois culture, most apparent in music and dance (see pages 99–100).

The main religion is Roman Catholicism, and many people are devoutly religious. But superstition – deriving largely from the beliefs of the African slaves – lives on. *Gris-gris* charms were (and perhaps still are) worn as protection against evil spirits and the evil eye. Despite the impact of the west and the growth of a modern economy, life is still fairly simple in some ways. Women no longer do their laundry in the river – it is discouraged and, anyway, many households now have washing machines – but you can still see washing spread out to dry on the grass,

Washing spread out to dry is a familiar sight in Seychelles

draped over bushes or even over gravestones in the old cemetery in Victoria. And women still like to use wash-day as an opportunity to exchange gossip.

The Seychellois Way of Life

'Stress' is not among the 3,000 words in the Creole vocabulary. If you let yourself relax, you will be beginning to adopt the Seychellois way of life.

Few Seychellois are workaholics. This does not mean that they are lazy, only that they like to enjoy life. A Seychellois would rather earn just enough to get by than work twice as hard to become a millionaire. It may take a while for the visitor from the rat-race to adjust to this attitude.

Nowadays the number of visitors a year is far greater than the total population of Seychelles, and the people have had to get used to this relatively recent influx of foreigners.

Fortunately, the Seychellois are friendly and hospitable. Householders are not allowed to offer rooms to let in their homes, so the chance for visitors to observe and share Seychellois family life are limited. However, most locals are pleased to show visitors round their homes, and friendships are easily made, sometimes leading to an invitation to dinner. Such opportunities should be grasped as a way of temporarily becoming a local – and also of enjoying authentic, home-cooked Creole food.

Seychellois society is not strait-laced – indeed the illegitimate birth rate is very high, and many couples leave the ritual of a wedding ceremony to romantically-inclined foreigners. Contraception *is* available, despite the ascendancy of the Roman Catholic church, to which 90 per cent of the population belongs. However, you may

see this message on a church in Bel Ombre on Mahé:
'Abortion and contraception are mortal sins. 5th day of every month is the day to prevent abortion (in all the world).'
In Seychelles, therefore, western visitors are not encountering a population likely to be too easily shocked by casual behaviour. Nevertheless, it is only courteous to dress discreetly when you go among people in towns and villages, where a swimsuit would not be regarded as adequate. Of course, on the more remote beaches and island resorts, casual dress is fine – but not nude sunbathing even here. Drunkenness, disorderly behaviour and rowdyism naturally cause offence.

CHILDREN

There is little risk in taking children, even babies, to Seychelles. The climate may affect some youngsters, but you cannot predict this.
Take all you might need for minor accidents or ailments and equip yourself against such things as heat rash or insect bites. Take a stock of nappies and other baby requisites, which are sold only in certain shops in Victoria: Antigone Trading in Victoria House and SMB Supermarket in Albert Street sell popular products.
The sun is the main danger to children, so ensure they wear a sunhat and plenty of sunscreen lotion or cream.

Most children have no problems with local food. Cereals are usually served in a breakfast buffet; the Beau-Vallon Bay Hotel is particularly recommended here. Ice-cream is best avoided as is tap water – stick to bottled water and soft drinks.
Many better class hotels provide baby-listening services. If this is important for the enjoyment of your stay, check with the hotel before booking.

Where to Stay
Beau Vallon Bay on Mahé and the Côte d'Or on Praslin are ideal for children. There are excellent beaches in both places and for older children there are paddle-skis, belly-boards, etc.
For those who prefer a quieter time, Bird Island and Silhouette are ideal for families. Note that several hotels, including Denis Island Lodge and Sunset Beach at Glacis on Mahé, do not accept children under 10.
Children's rates vary. For instance, at the Coral Strand (Beau Vallon), children of 2-12 years stay free if sharing with parents and there is 50 per cent discount on their meal prices. Rates at the Equator (Grand'Anse, Mahé) are: children of 2-12 free if sharing with two adults in the low season and up to 75 per cent of the applicable adult rate at peak times (July-August and December). A child occupying a third bed in a room with parents stays free at the Auberge Louis XVII (Mahé).

What to Do

Glass-bottom boat trips, excursions to Sainte Anne Marine National Park off Mahé, snorkelling and nature walks are all ideal occupations for children. And, of course, the beaches are wonderful playgrounds (but remember that collecting shells is illegal). Youngsters also love riding in the ox-carts on La Digue. Entertaining children may not be easy if it rains. The Beau-Vallon Bay Hotel has a well equipped games and video room for such an eventuality.

TIGHT BUDGET

Seychelles is emphatically not for budget-travellers. Almost everything is imported so the cost of living is high – higher still in the outer islands. Even lager brewed in Mahé costs more than an equivalent pint in London, Sydney or New York. Dining out is marginally cheaper, but it becomes costly to eat out every night. There are few cheap snack bars on Mahé and none elsewhere. An electric travel-jug with a supply of tea-bags will save some costs.

There are no cheap return air-fares to Mahé from Europe. A ticket to Seychelles costs as much as a return trip from London to Sydney. The only answer for travellers with a limited budget is a package tour. There are packages offering guesthouse accommodation on a bed and breakfast basis which are considerably cheaper than a deal offering half board in a

Sub-sea viewer

first class hotel. On top of that, you still have to eat and drink – and budget for excursions or car rental, which can be expensive.

Independent travellers should budget for spending three to four times more than in, say, India or Malaysia. Carried away by romance, many honeymooners return home broke. If you wish to budget against the odds stay in guesthouses.

If you are hoping to stay in guesthouses note that this kind of accommodation is always booked up in advance. If you arrive expecting to find somewhere cheap to stay you will almost certainly be disappointed. Cheap private rooms are not available. However, there is nothing to stop a second-time visitor to Seychelles taking advantage of an invitation to stay from a friend made on the first visit. Sleeping rough is not allowed, and even camping is illegal. Eating out can be expensive. There are no mass fast-food outlets like McDonalds, and no take-aways outside Victoria (there are only two or three there). Most guesthouses serve a full English breakfast, so you can skip lunch and fill up at dinner. **Marie-Antoinette Restaurant** in Victoria offers good-value meals. Otherwise buy picnic food.

There is no cheap means of travel in Seychelles other than public buses. Car rental is expensive. At present you can rent a bicycle only on La Digue. Keen cyclists should enquire the cost of bringing their own cycles but you still face the cost of interisland ferries. To visit Silhouette, a lovely island 70 minutes from Mahé, costs more than a return crossing of the English Channel. Outer islands are only linked by air. In short there is no way round Seychelles on the cheap. Backpackers are conspicuously absent.

If you still wish to budget against the odds:

- buy a budget package tour, or
- book guesthouse accommodation well in advance
- stay bed and breakfast
- shop around for cheap restaurants
- buy simple picnic lunches
- make your duty-free allowance of alcohol last – many hotels charge

exorbitantly for those tempting cocktails.

SPECIAL EVENTS

Every village in Seychelles celebrates its own saint's day. These days are, of course, not public holidays, and are too numerous to list here. However, if you happen to encounter one, it is a colourful occasion. The following are the principal general festivals:

New Year (31 December/ 1 January)
New Year is celebrated more than Christmas. Parties go on from New Year's Eve through into New Year's Day. People like to go from house to house offering good wishes.

Liberation Day (5 June)
This is the main official day of celebration in Seychelles. It commemorates the ousting of the first government of the independent Republic on 5 June 1977, and the coming to power of Albert René. There are processions and various activities in all the islands.

Assumption Day (15 August)
This is an important religious festival, celebrated in particular on the island of La Digue, where it is called 'Lafet Kreol'. In addition to a religious procession, there are sports and competitions.

Immaculate Conception (8 December)
The festival is best observed in Victoria, where a religious procession, with the statue of the Virgin Mary, goes through the streets of the capital.

SPORT

The most popular activities in Seychelles are watersports – windsurfing, fishing, sailing, diving and so on. Land sports include tennis and golf.

Diving

Diving is possible all year round, but seasonal changes affect water temperature and visibility. April–May and October–November are the best diving times. The ocean is calm and visibility may extend to 100 feet (30m). Water temperature frequently reaches 29°C (84°F) but on deep dives, a wetsuit is recommended.

Diving is mainly from a boat although some places offer shore-dives. Diving on inshore coral reefs varies between 30 and 60 feet (10 and 20m) to a maximum of 100 feet (30m). Most diving centres offer a choice of dives including wrecks, night dives or 'adventure dives' in more remote areas known by locals. You do not need to bring any special equipment as all diving centres are fully equipped with weights, wetsuits and flippers as well as scuba, depth gauges, etc. If you bring gear it must be seen to work properly and you must dive with a BCD, or similar power inflation mechanism. You must also use a contents gauge. Most diving centres can correct any minor faults in equipment. If you are a qualified diver, remember your log-book. There is a portable decompression chamber in Victoria, but the nearest full decompression facilities are in Mombasa, Kenya. Holiday insurance policies may require an extra premium for divers.

Learning to Dive

There are several diving centres on Mahé, Praslin and Desroches where you can learn to dive (see page 108 for details). Monitors speak English, German, Italian and French. Most are members of the Association of Professional Divers and are fully qualified teachers. People in possession of a 'Funcard' from Seychelles Hotels (see page 44) get a free introductory dive.

The first course, a tutorial, explains the effects of diving and essential safety procedures. A session in the swimming-pool follows to learn basic skills – clearing your mask underwater, how to surface and so on. When you

A diving lesson at the Coral Strand Hotel, Beau Vallon Beach, Mahé

SPORT

feel confident, the centre will take you out for a dive on the reefs. A full diving licence, recognised worldwide, requires five days' intensive certification courses including four open-water dives. Smart, fit beginners can pick up diving basics in a day. The diving centres at Northolme Hotel on Mahé and the Praslin Beach Watersports Centre are well regarded.

Fitness
First-time divers must complete a medical questionnaire at one of the centres. Providing you are fit, not prone to epilepsy and are not taking medication you should be okay. If uncertain, get a fitness clearance from your doctor before going on holiday. Women should not dive during pregnancy.

It is important to remember you should have a full 24-hour break after diving before you fly.

Diving Centres
Diving in Paradise, Praslin Beach Hotel, Watersports Centre, Anse Volbert, Praslin (tel: 32148).

Seychelles Underwater Centre, Coral Strand Hotel, PO Box 384, Mahé (tel: 47357).

Marine Divers, Northolme Hotel, PO Box 333, Mahé (tel: 47589).

Underwater Photography
If it is hard enough taking good photos in changing surface conditions, it is more difficult under water. Here you have to confront cold, currents, poor visibility, loss of colour, and unpredictably moving subjects.

You can take reasonable underwater photographs snorkelling from the surface, but the best are obtained with scuba. Assuming you are a certified diver with a reasonable camera, you can start filming.

Loss of colour is the biggest problem, as water filters out light. Red disappears at only 13-16 feet (4-5m), orange by 26 feet (8m) and yellow at 36 feet (11m); blue goes at 72 feet (22m) and by 100 feet (30m) everything is grey.

Although it is expensive, the best plan is to take several different exposures. For close-ups of reef life obtain a meter reading of your subject and use an appropriate flashlight exposure.

A good standard 35mm lens, aperture 3.5-22, gives good results to within a metre. A 28mm lens has excellent depth of field which is very important in undersea photography. Choose as slow a film as you dare, dependent on what depth you are going to work in. However, do not expect to get good pictures on your first diving holiday.

Fishing
The Seychelles archipelago offers unlimited fishing potential. The only places where fishing is illegal are off Cousin and Sainte Anne Marine National Park. You can buy fishing equipment in Victoria, but it is better to bring everything you may need, including spares. For

Game-fishing off Denis Island

beach, rock and boat fishing, a
medium-lightweight fibreglass
rod and Mitchell-type reel are
recommended. Hooks and line
obviously depend on where
you fish and what you are
hoping to catch.

Bait varies from crabs and
shellfish to fresh fish. Bonito is
sure-fire. Where possible,
most keen anglers catch their
bait: you could try fishing for
garfish with a float and fresh
prawn. Needlefish are
common and equally
successful bait. Grab them
behind the head on landing –
they bite savagely. Small fresh
mullet are good for in-shore
angling. Schools swim among
tidal mangroves around Port
Glaud, and lagoons on
Silhouette. Squid are excellent
all-round bait if you can catch
one.

Fishing, like other watersports,
is limited by the prevailing
wind. The best plan is to
enquire about where to fish
from an old Seychellois
fisherman. Grand'Anse on
Mahé offers good mixed
fishing from parrot fish to
shark.

If renting a boat, ensure you
carry an anchor, oars, drinking
water and flares. Two
Englishmen, lost off Mahé in
July 1990, carried nothing for
an emergency. Test the motor
before you leave.

Deep-sea Fishing
Game-fishermen require a
quality product and are willing
to pay for it. It cannot be said
that Seychelles can compete
on a pro-rata basis with other
renowned deep-sea fishing
spots. The fish are there, but
organisation is generally
unsophisticated. Local
fishermen are casual about
equipment and often troll too
fast with the bait bouncing out
of the water. They give an
impression of local know-how,
but even off Île Denis –
renowned for game-fishing –
they could catch more than
they do. You pay high rates for
the rich man's sport of game-
fishing so insist the boatman
fishes how you want. Gear is
supplied on charters. Rates
per rod vary from boat to boat.
Bait – usually bonito – is
supplied.

For big-game fishing charters:
apply to **Marine Charter
Association**, Victoria Harbour,
Mahé (tel: 22126).

Hotels on Praslin, La Digue,
Bird, Denis and Desroches
offer deep-sea fishing trips.
The water off the Seychelles
Bank around Bird and Denis is
rich in bill-fish, *wahoo*, *mahi-*

SPORT

mahi, dogtooth tuna, kingfish, dorado and mackerel.

Golf
Barbarons hotel-guests on the west coast of Mahé can pitch and putt on the grandly named Beoliere Country Golfcourse. There is a tropical-style, 9-hole course opposite the Reef Hotel at Anse aux Pins on Mahé's east side (tel: 76251). A mangrove swamp is one of the hazards, and crabs sometimes take the balls. A notice warns against falling coconuts. There is a small club-house with caddies available by prior arrangement. Visitors are welcome.

Paragliding
'Leisure 2000' at Beau Vallon Bay on Mahé are specialists in paragliding (as well as watersports). Monitors are certified by the American Parascending Association. Children as young as eight can paraglide with a teacher.
Leisure 2000 Watersports: Box 381, Victoria. Contact Coral Strand Hotel (tel: 47036) for information.

Riding
Horses are few and far between in Seychelles. Rides through the wooded hills overlooking Anse Boileau on Mahé can sometimes be arranged through the Barbarons (tel: 72339 or 78577).

Sailing
Yachts and sailing boats can be hired by the hour, or day, from the Yacht Club in Victoria (tel: 22126). Temporary membership can be arranged; there is a cafeteria and cruising yacht notice-board. Considerable sailing expertise is essential during the southeast trade winds. Simple sailing boats (dinghies, catamarans, etc) can be hired at most hotels. Beau Vallon Bay is a good family-type sailing spot. Canoes, belly-boards and paddle-skis are available from watersports centres.

Tennis
Many hotels on Mahé have tennis courts. You can even play tennis in the outer islands, notably on Île Denis. Some of the best courts – at the Reef, Equator and Meridien Barbarons hotels – are floodlit.

Water-skiing
Seychelles is not renowned for water-skiing. At certain times of the year it can be organised at Beau Vallon Bay on Mahé. Water-scooters are available for rent.

Windsurfing
Windsurfing is popular in Seychelles. There are learning centres on Mahé, at Beau Vallon Bay and Anse aux Pins by the Reef Hotel. Praslin is another windsurfing centre. There are problems. Southeast trade winds blow in gusts which make it very hard to control the sail, while on the lee side of an island, you have no wind at all. Windsurfing in shallow water over the coral reefs needs good experience. Only accomplished windsurfers should tackle the lagoon off Silhouette Island. In the right wind, Beau Vallon Bay and Côte d'Or on Praslin are best.

DIRECTORY

Arriving

Seychelles International Airport on Mahé opened to international flights in 1971. It is now served by more than half a dozen overseas airlines. British Airways and Air Seychelles are the main operators from the United Kingdom, but connections can also be made on Air France, Alitalia and Kenya Airways from Paris, Rome and Nairobi.
Air Seychelles: the national flag-carrier is highly recommended. It operates a Boeing 767 service three times a week from London Gatwick to Mahé, via Paris, Frankfurt or Rome. Flight time is about 11 hours. Passenger capacity is 196 in economy and 12 in 'Pearl Class'. Cabin crew are warm, well groomed and professional, speaking English, French, Creole, Spanish, German and Italian.
Air Seychelles Ltd, Head Office: Victoria House, PO Box 386, Mahé, Seychelles (tel: 21400).

Seychelles:
International Reservations: Victoria House, Mahé (tel: 21547/8).
Australia: General Sales Agents International Pty Ltd, Melbourne: tel: (03) 429 6522;

Local children in Victoria

DIRECTORY

Sydney: tel (02) 296 832;
Perth: tel (09) 481 211;
Brisbane: tel (07) 846 2629.
Canada: 587a Yung Street,
Ontario, Canada M4Y 124
(tel: (416) 922-690).
UK: Suite 6, Kelvin House,
Kelvin Way, Crawley, West
Sussex RH10 2SE
(tel: (0293) 536313).
US: APS Inc North America,
5777 West Century Boulevard,
Suite 875, Los Angeles,
California CA-90045-5631
(tel: (213) 670-7302).

**Seychelles International
Airport** is on the main island of
Mahé, 20 minutes' drive from
the capital, Victoria; nearest
hotel is the Reef at Anse aux
Pins. The airport is clean and
comfortable with WCs, banks,
a shop selling stamps and
phone-cards, a post-box and
international and local
telephone facilities. There is a
restaurant selling snacks plus
non-alcoholic drinks and
coffee. There are also left
luggage facilities, taxis, rent-a-
car desk and free baggage
trolleys. Porters are available
– a tip is not expected, but any
small change is always
appreciated.
Praslin Airport is small, clean
and comfortable with taxi and
rent-a-car facilities, WC, café
with snacks, drinks, books and
souvenirs. It is 25 minutes'
drive from main resort area,
Côte d'Or. Closest hotel is
Maison des Palmes,
Grand'Anse.
Other island airports are
merely runways with no
facilities. Handling is by local
hotel staff.

There are no airport departure
taxes in Seychelles.

Entry Formalities
All visitors require a valid
passport. An embarkation form
is handed out on Air
Seychelles flights on which you
must state the purpose, length,
etc of your visit. On arrival,
immigration officials grant
entry for one month. You
should have available, if
required, valid travel
documents and proof of
sufficient funds. Anyone not in
possession of an
onward/return ticket may be
asked to deposit the equivalent
sum of money. Queries should
be directed to: the
**Immigration Officer,
Immigration & Civil Status
Division, Ministry of
Administration and
Manpower, PO Box 430,
Victoria, Mahé.**

Camping
Camping is illegal in all the
islands.

Chemist
(see **Pharmacies**)

Crime
There is no serious crime
against the person in
Seychelles, which is especially
safe for women visitors. Mahé
and Praslin, however, have an
appalling rate of theft. The
police's success rate in
tracking down offenders is
low. Your property is at risk
from the moment you arrive.
Never leave anything in a
vehicle, or unattended on the
beach. Make use of hotel safe
deposit facilities for your
money and small valuables.

A Mini-Moke, ideal for exploring

Keep anything else of value locked in your suitcase. Locals have a special predilection for cameras, but personal jewellery can be worn without too much risk.

Customs Regulations

Visitors may bring in duty free: 125ml perfume, 250ml toilet water, 200 cigarettes or 250g tobacco, 1 litre spirits and 1 litre wine. Firearms and spearguns are illegal. Customs officers are polite and efficient; they will usually request you to open one suitcase.
A certificate of export is necessary for the coco-de-mer.

Disabled People

There are no specific deals for disabled travellers to Seychelles, and many of the excursions are fairly gruelling. However, a beach holiday in bungalow accommodation is a possibility.

Driving

In Seychelles driving is on the left and follows British rules. Mahé has about 95 miles (150km) of tarred road and some 70 miles (110km) of bumpy dirt tracks. On Mahé, the speed limit is 25mph (40km/h) in built-up areas. Elsewhere 40mph (65km/h). The local speed limit is 25mph (40km/h) on Praslin. These are the only islands with motor traffic.
The narrow coast road winding around Mahé has deep gutters or a steep drop with no footpaths. Pedestrians are a considerable hazard. Be especially careful when schools come out at 14.30hrs, and on Saturday afternoon and evening when you may encounter drunks. Try not to drive at night. Traffic is light, but there are no street-lights outside Victoria.

Breakdown Service

There is none. Obtain the

DIRECTORY

house number of the manager of your rent-a-car company before setting off. Call him in an emergency. Accustomed to problems, most respond promptly.

Car Rental

To rent a car no international driving licence is required, but you should hold a licence valid in your own country. Drivers are required to be over 21 and to have held a licence for two years.

Car-hire is a buyer's market if you care to bargain. Most Mini-Mokes (the standard rented vehicle) are in a lamentable state, as they come in and are rented straight out again without a check. Flat tyres are common, hand-brakes rarely work and your Moke may have no rear vision mirror. As parts are hard to obtain and life expectancy is regulated by the government to three years, owners show no concern for safety. If you are British, a licence is not always required as proof you can drive. Mini-Mokes are unsuitable if you have more than one suitcase, as anything loose will fly out on the bends. The tiny box at the rear may not have a padlock so take a lock with you in anticipation. Articles left on the seats disappear in seconds. Some exotically named local companies offer more competitive rates than the big names (check the car-hire desk at Mahé Airport and see list below).

Alpha Rent-a-car, Victoria (tel: 22078).
Avis, Victoria, (tel: 24511).

Budget Rent-a-car, Victoria (tel: 44280).
City Car Hire, Anse aux Pins (tel: 76829).
Eden's Cars, St Louis Road, above Victoria (tel: 23359).
Europcar/InterRent, Victoria and Beau Vallon (tel: 23303).
Hertz Leisure Car Hire, Victoria (tel: 22447/22669).
Ideal Car Rental, Les Mamelles (tel: 44280).
Joe's Car Hire, Airport, Beau Vallon (tel: 23420).
Kobe Cars, Victoria (tel: 21888).
MS Car Rental, Victoria (tel: 76522).
Mein's Car Hire, St Louis (tel: 23005).
National Travel Agency, Victoria (tel: 24900).
Nelson's Car Hire, St Louis (tel: 22923).
Petit Car Hire, Victoria (tel: 44608).
Ram Car Hire, Victoria (tel: 23443).
St Louis Motor Hire, St Louis Hill (tel: 22270).
Sunshine Cars, Victoria (tel: 24671).
Tropicar, Mont Fleuri (tel: 23838).
Union Vale Car Hire, Beau Vallon Road (tel: 47052).
Victoria Car Hire, Anse aux Pins (tel: 76314).
Car-Hire Operator's Association: Victoria (tel: 24547).

Praslin has a limited number of 'Mokes' and 'Suzukis', and it is wise to book a vehicle during peak holiday periods. All island hotels can order a rent-a-car, or arrange one to meet your flight at the airport.

Car rental firms include:
Austral, Bay Sainte Anne
(tel: 32015).
Echo, Amitié (tel: 33826).
Praslin Holiday Co,
Grand'Anse (tel: 33219).
Prestige, Grand'Anse
(tel: 33226).
Solace, Grand'Anse
(tel: 33525).
Standard, Anse Kerlan
(tel: 33555).

Fuel

Most rental operators put 5
litres of petrol in your car, and
it should be returned containing
the same amount. It is advisable
to fill up as soon as possible, as
filling stations are few and far
between. Fuel stations are
found at: the International
Airport, Beau Vallon, Anse aux
Pins, and outside the Sheraton,
Port Glaud. Stations give good
service.
Seychelles Petroleum, Mahé
(tel: 24240).

Parking

You may park for 20 minutes in
the spaces provided in
Victoria. Public car parks are
found behind the Pirate's
Arms, near the National
Library and at the end of State
Avenue. There are no
charges.

Drugs

Illegal possession of drugs,
from cannabis up, carries a jail
sentence of up to 15 years.

Electricity

The electric current is usually
240 AC via three-point plugs
with square pins. A torch is
essential wherever you go at
night. Even the main road past
Beau Vallon Bay, on Mahé, has
no street lights. Take spare
torch batteries. The
lightweight, waterproof torches
sold at AA outlets are
recommended.

Embassies and Consulates

US Embassy, Victoria House,
Mahé (tel: 23921).
British High Commission,
Victoria House, Mahé
(tel: 23055/23056).

Emergency Telephone Numbers

Fire, police, ambulance: 999
Seychelles Hospital, Mont
Fleuri, Mahé (all hours):
tel: 24400. For dental and eye
problems and communicable
diseases.
For emergencies on other
islands, consult reception at
your hotel or guesthouse or the
local administrator.

Entry Formalities
(see **Arriving**).

Entertainment Information

Current entertainments are
listed in the *Seychelles Nation*,
the daily newspaper. Also on
hotel bulletin boards; through
travel agency representatives
who are on duty at all tourist
hotels; and through
publications of the tourist office
which are distributed to hotels
on Mahé.

Health

Seychelles is free from malaria
and other tropical diseases. No
vaccination certificates are
therefore necessary, but keep
your tetanus and polio
immunisation up to date.
You should pack a medical kit
containing disinfectant, cotton-
wool, plasters, lotions for bites

and stings (and antihistamines if you suffer severe allergic reactions), anti-diarrhoeal tablets and analgesics. *Do not forget it on interisland travels*. If you cannot treat your complaint yourself, see a doctor at the local hospital or clinic. Charges for hospital visits are payable before you leave. If a doctor visits your hotel his fee can be paid at the same time as your hotel bill. Obtain receipts in order to make insurance claims.

Bites and Stings
Mosquitoes and sandflies can make life unpleasant, particularly on Praslin. Hotels usually supply coils and nets. Include a good repellent in your medical kit: 'Repel 1000' is recommended. Sandflies bite where seaweed lies on the beach. Scratching may cause an infection which leaves an ulcer.

It is a precaution to check your bedding for unwanted bed-fellows.

Jelly-fish and the odd bluebottle can cause painful stings. Such unfortunate happenings may occur on the outer coral islands; whisky applied to the affected area will ease the pain.

Colds and Flu
Foreign visitors sometimes catch terrible chills from sleeping with the air-conditioning on. This is dangerous in a tropical climate. Turn it off before you go to bed.

Diarrhoea
To safeguard against diarrhoea, drink only bottled

mineral water and avoid ice and sorbets. You are still likely to suffer an upset stomach somewhere on Mahé. If it does not clear up in a day or two, see a local doctor.

Insurance
The Seychelles government provides all available medical services to visitors – this means you pay a doctor's consulting fee and for all prescribed medication. A helicopter can be provided for anyone seriously ill or injured in the outer islands.

The Tourist Office strongly recommends a standard health and insurance policy be taken out. Tourists who book with a tour operator can buy coverage through the operator. Read the policy carefully to ascertain you have adequate cover which will depend on your personal state of health, the value of your belongings etc. Make sure you keep the receipts of any 'holiday buys'. In the event of loss, you will need to send these with an insurance claim. Health care is excellent in Seychelles, but it must be paid for on the spot and reimbursement claimed on your return home.

Personal Necessities
Take a supply of earplugs, condoms, tampons, sanitary towels or babies' nappies. Even analgesics are not always readily available. Condoms can be obtained from the family planning clinic at Mont Fleuri Hospital. For other pharmaceutical items try the **SMB Supermarket** in Albert

Street or **Antigone Traders** in Victoria House in Victoria, Mahé.

Sea-urchins and Coral Cuts

Sea-urchins are a hazard in many popular snorkelling areas. Urine sponged on the wounds will draw out broken spines. Do not handle 'fire coral' which causes painful, red weals. Wear gym-shoes or plastic sandals for walking on exposed reefs. Do not pick up cone shells whose sting may be fatal.

Sexually Transmitted Diseases

These are not yet a serious problem in Seychelles. AIDS is still rare. If you think you may have caught something, go to the outpatients department of hospital, where minor conditions can be treated.

Sunburn

Listen to what the experts advise about skin cancer. You are not safe exposing yourself to the sun, so do not go outside without covering yourself in a cream, milk or lotion with a high sun protection factor – at least 15, preferably 20. Wear a hat and sunglasses at all times.

Treatment

Seychelles Hospital, Mont Fleuri, Mahé (tel: 24400). Open 24 hours for casualties.
Baie Sainte Anne Hospital, Praslin (tel: 33333).
Vallée de Mai road (right hand turn, two minutes' drive from Baie Sainte Anne).

Holidays
Religious

Good Friday and Easter weekend; 5 June: Corpus Christi; 15 August: Assumption Day – special festivities on La Digue; 1 November: All Saints' Day; 8 December: Festival of the Immaculate Conception; 25 December: Christmas Day.

Public

1-2 January: New Year; 1 May: Labour Day; 5 June: Liberation Day; 29 June: celebrated as a national sports day, especially in Victoria Stadium.

Lost Property

You can wave goodbye to anything attractive you may have lost. If you report a loss, obtain a police copy of the report for insurance claims. Airport and hotel left luggage facilities are safe.

Marrying in Seychelles

Couples may get married in Seychelles at a civil ceremony which is recognised by many countries as legal. The ceremony, which can take place on Mahé only, is conducted by the Registrar. There are two ways to arrange

Weddings are a booming business

DIRECTORY

a wedding in Seychelles. The first – and by far the simplest – is to book through a tour operator offering a wedding option in addition to the normal holiday package. A supplement is payable, and not all operators' arrangements are identical. Check the individual operator's brochure for exact details and costs.

Alternatively, a couple may make arrangements directly with the Registrar, at the Civil Status Office, PO Box 430, Victoria, Mahé, Seychelles, allowing at least two months to process the documentation and make the necessary arrangements. You should advise him of the dates of your visit, the name of your hotel where the ceremony will take place, and a preferred date (give alternative dates). The hotel must also confirm that the chosen date is acceptable, and advise a suitable time.

Also send photocopies of both birth certificates, any applicable divorce papers (decree absolute) and copies of the first six pages of each passport.

A couple must normally be in Seychelles for 11 days before the wedding, when no licence fee is payable. In any other case, there is a special licence fee of SR100.

The Registrar will confirm whether he is available to perform the wedding, give fee details and say if documentation is required. All details should be clearly confirmed in writing well in advance of departure, to avoid any disappointment, or misunderstanding. When booking through a tour operator, couples should clarify exactly what is covered by the supplement payable, and what is optional (eg photography, cake, music, etc) and normally payable in the resort.

Air Seychelles advises that wedding dresses should be carried in garment bags, and not in large dress boxes, which cannot be accommodated on the aircraft.

Media
Newspapers and Magazines

The *Seychelles Nation*, published Monday to Saturday in English, French and Creole, is on sale early in shops, police stations and hotels. It contains currency rates, airline movements, shipping and weather details and overseas news briefs. International papers arrive a day late and sell quickly from the **Space** bookshop, Huteau Lane, and **National Bookshop** on Albert Street, Victoria. British and French newspapers are available at the National Library. *Seychelles Today* is a glossy English-French quarterly magazine with interesting features on local life – the economy, culture, nature, personalities.

Radio Seychelles

Broadcasts on 219 metres, 1368khz Monday to Friday 06.30-08.00, 11.00-13.15 and 18.00-22.00hrs. Weekend transmissions from 06.30-22.00hrs. English news at 19.00hrs.

RTS – Radio Television Seychelles
Broadcasts an excellent half-hour coverage of local and overseas news in English at 18.00, Creole at 19.00 and French at 20.30hrs.

Money Matters

One Seychelles rupee = 100 cents. Notes are for 10, 25, 50 and 100 rupees. Coins are in denominations of 1, 5, 10 and 25 cents. Exchange rates are published daily in the local paper. Travellers' cheques command a better rate than cash. There are banking facilities at the International Airport, open for all arrivals and departures. Rates are considerably better than in hotels.

Large hotels, car rental companies and most big shops accept credit cards. Interisland flights may also be paid for by credit card. Praslin, La Digue, Denis and Bird islands recognise major credit cards. They are not acceptable on Silhouette.

Banks

Barclays Bank PLC, Independence Avenue, PO Box 167, Victoria (tel: 24101).
Banque Française Commerciale, O.I., PO Box 122, Victoria (tel: 23096).
Standard Chartered Bank, Kingsgate House, Independence Avenue, PO Box 241, Victoria (tel: 25011).
Habib Bank Ltd, Francis Rachel Street, PO Box 702, Victoria (tel: 24371).
Bank of Baroda, Albert Street, PO Box 124, Victoria (tel: 23038).

Seychelles currency

Bank of Credit & Commerce Int SA, Victoria House, PO Box 579, Victoria (tel: 22303/22305).
Seychelles Saving Bank, PO Box 531, Independence House, Victoria (tel: 25251).

Opening Times
Banks
Most banks are open Monday to Friday 08.30-13.30hrs, Saturday 08.30-11.00hrs.

Businesses
Generally open Monday to Friday 08.00-16.00hrs.

Shops
Generally open Monday to Friday 08.00-17.00hrs., and 08.00-12.00hrs. on Saturday. Some traders open on Sunday mornings.

Personal Safety
Travellers in Seychelles are safer than in most parts of the world. A woman travelling alone, should not suffer harassment providing she observes the ground-rules, like not sunbathing alone on a deserted beach or walking about on her own at night.

DIRECTORY

Preparing coco-de-mer fronds at the Village Artisanal, Mahé

Most prohibited areas are out of bounds, because they are protected nature reserves (Aldabra is an example). North of Port Glaud on Mahé is a restricted military area. But there are few places one may not go. All are indicated by signs in all main languages. See also **Crime**.

Pharmacies

Behram's Pharmacy, Mont Fleuri, Mahé near Harbour View Guesthouse (tel: 23659).
Fock-Heng Pharmacy, Revolution Avenue, Victoria (tel: 22751).
Central Chemist, Mont Fleuri Hospital is open 08.00-18.00hrs. Monday to Friday and weekends 08.00-12.00hrs.
Antigone Trading and **SMB Supermarket** in Victoria sell pharmaceutical requirements.

Photography

You will find certain problems in taking good pictures. Dazzling white beaches can confuse an automatic exposure camera. It may also balk at taking black and white in the one exposure. Weather is another worry. You may be using slow film for bright sun, when the sky abruptly turns grey.

Keen photographers should keep handy several film-speeds. Fujichrome 50 ASA or Kodachrome 64 ASA are excellent in bright light. Alternatively, use up to 100-200 ASA and do not forget your flash in the shady Vallée de Mai on Praslin (see page 56). Standard print film can be developed in a day or two in Victoria with reasonable results.

Bird Photography

Check your camera regularly for sand grains, and pack it in a plastic bag on boat trips. Flashlights are not permitted near nesting birds on Cousin and you cannot expect good results in the shadowy foliage. A 135mm lens is adequate for the sooty tern colony on Bird Island. Birds on the wing may need a 200-300mm lens.

Places of Worship

There are Anglican and Roman Catholic cathedrals in Victoria. Every village on Mahé and Praslin has a parish church (mainly Roman Catholic). Churches and chapels are also found on La Digue, Frégate, Silhouette, Denis and Moyenne. Check service times with your hotel

or guesthouse.
There are no synagogues.

Police

Policemen in Mahé wear British-style uniforms but sighting one is a rare experience. On the outer islands, law is maintained by a visiting officer, and, where called for, by a visiting judge and prosecutor.

Central Police Station:, Victoria, Mahé (tel: 22011).
Other Police Stations: Mont Fleuri (tel: 22011); Beau Vallon, Mahé (tel: 47242); Anse Royale, Mahé (tel: 71226); Grand'Anse, Praslin (tel: 33251); La Digue (tel: 34251).

Post Office

The central post office is at Independence Avenue, Victoria, open Monday to Friday 08.00-16.00hrs and Saturday 08.00-12.00hrs. Shops selling postcards usually also sell stamps. There is a letter-box at the airport. Allow five days for mail to Europe; 8 to 14 days to Australia or the US.

Public Transport

Buses

Mahé: an unpunctual bus service operates daily on Mahé 05.30-19.00hrs (locals waiting on the road are grateful for a lift). Buses have standing room only at peak hours – 07.00-09.00 and 16.00-17.00hrs, and are driven at considerable speed. Travel agencies run 18-seater coaches for airport and ferry transfers (cost included on package tours).
Praslin: The island's bus service operates from 05.30-19.00hrs. on the main routes. There is a special Sunday service. There is a bus service from Grand'Anse to Côte d'Or via the Vallée de Mai. There is a timetable at the airport and in many hotels.

Taxis

Taxis are normally ordered at your hotel or picked up at the airport, but it is unlikely a driver would refuse to stop if hailed. There are set prices for all distances so if you do hail a cab, confirm the rate before setting off.
Mahé has plenty of comfortable metered taxis. Ranks are found at the International Airport and on Albert Street, Victoria. A waiting rank is found outside the larger hotels. Hiring a taxi with driver-guide works out good value for a day's excursion on Mahé. Drivers are enthusiastic.
Taxi Operators Association: Olivier Mardin Street, Victoria, Mahé (tel: 23895).
Praslin: There is a taxi-rank at Praslin Airport. Taxis also meet the interisland ferries. Taxis are always found at the larger hotels.
Taxiphone: Amitié Airstrip – tel: 33429; Baie Sainte Anne jetty – tel: 33859.

Interisland Air Transport

Air Seychelles operates frequent daily services by Britten-Norman Islander (nine seats) and Twin Otter (20 seats) from Mahé to Praslin. First departure is 05.40 hrs; last flight ex-Praslin 19.05hrs. Check-in 30 minutes before departure at Interisland

DIRECTORY

terminal on Mahé, adjacent to the International Airport. It offers excellent handling, a clean WC and a small shop. Special daily charters operate to Frégate, Denis, Bird and Desroches. Scenic flights are available off Mahé: 30 minutes' duration.

Baggage: this is limited to one item of normally not more than 10 kilos due to the payload of small aircraft. Heavier items may be deposited at Left Luggage, International Airport (within walking distance). Non-essential luggage is best left at your hotel. Air Seychelles adopts a lenient approach on baggage to people making direct international connections from the islands.

Flight-times: Mahé–Praslin 15 minutes; Mahé–Bird 30 minutes; Mahé–Denis 30 minutes; Mahé–Frégate 15 minutes; Mahé–Desroches 60 minutes.

Air Seychelles links the islands

Interisland Enquiries: Seychelles International Airport (tel: 73101).

Interisland Ferry Transport Privately owned schooners operate regular connections Mahé–Praslin–La Digue. Details as follows (subject to change):

Schedule 1: Baie Sainte Anne, Praslin to Mahé and return
La Belle Praslinoise: Monday, Wednesday and Friday, depart Praslin 05.30 arrive Mahé 08.30hrs; depart Mahé 11.00, arrive Praslin 14.00hrs.
Cousin: Tuesday, Thursday, depart Praslin 06.00, arrive Mahé 08.30hrs; depart Mahé 12.00, arrive Praslin 14.30hrs. Monday and Wednesday depart Praslin 06.00 and 06.30, arrive Mahé 08.00 and 08.30hrs. Depart Mahé both days 13.00, arrive Praslin 15.30hrs.
La Bellone: Monday depart Praslin 05.30, arrive Mahé 08.30hrs; depart Mahé 11.00, arrive Praslin 14.00hrs.

Schedule 2: La Digue–Mahé and Mahé–La Digue
La Belle Edna: Monday, Wednesday and Friday depart La Digue 06.00, arrive Mahé 09.15hrs; depart Mahé 13.00, arrive La Digue 16.15 hrs. Tuesday and Thursday depart La Digue 06.00, arrive Mahé 09.15hrs; depart Mahé 12.00, arrive La Digue 15.15hrs.

Schedule 3: Baie Sainte Anne, Praslin to La Digue and La Digue to Praslin
Silhouette: Monday and Tuesday depart Praslin 07.00, arrive La Digue 07.30hrs; depart La Digue 07.30, arrive Praslin 08.00hrs; Wednesday depart Praslin 09.30, arrive La Digue 10.00hrs; depart La Digue 10.00, arrive Praslin 10.30hrs. Thursday depart Praslin 10.30, arrive La Digue 11.00hrs; depart La Digue 11.30, arrive Praslin 12.00hrs.
Lady Mary: Friday depart Praslin 14.30, arrive La Digue 15.00hrs; depart La Digue 15.30, arrive Praslin 16.00hrs. Saturday depart Praslin 17.00, arrive La Digue 17.30hrs, depart La Digue 17.30, arrive Praslin 18.00hrs.

Yacht Charters
Rates for yacht charter vary according to the number of passengers, size of vessel and how far you wish to go. From two to four people the cost is about SR2,500 per day in immediate waters. Chartering an eight-person sailing vessel to visit the Amirantes costs from SR10,000 per day. Departures and enquiries: **Marine Charter**, PO Box 469, Victoria, Mahé (tel: 22126).

Senior Citizens
Choice of hotel is particularly important for older visitors to Seychelles. Access to the beach and swimming-pool is often down steep steps. On Mahé, the **Plantation Club** is ideal. Also recommended is the **Paradise Hotel** on Praslin, and **Île Denis**. Older tourists may find the heat oppressive during November-December. Certain excursions such as Moyenne, Cousin and the Vallée de Mai on Praslin are unsuitable unless you are a fit walker. Medical facilities are limited outside Victoria and there is an apparent lack of comfortable deck chairs in the Seychelles.

Student and Youth Travel
The cost of living is beyond most student budgets. Cost of accommodation and food on top of the already expensive air-fare, limits Seychelles to well-heeled holidaymakers. If anywhere, La Digue is the best bet for young tourists. Bicycles may be rented, but there is still a shortage of cheap hotels and restaurants. It is possible to hitch-hike on Mahé and Praslin.

Telephones
Seychelles has one of the best telecommunications systems in the world. Even the outer islands are linked by phone and FAX. *Publiphone* boxes are found in strategic places on Mahé, Praslin and La Digue. All large hotels operate a direct dial service. You will pay a much higher rate for any call made via the operator. Phone-cards may be used for

DIRECTORY

international calls at Seychelles Airport – available from the shop.

To call Seychelles from abroad, dial the Seychelles country code (248) preceded by the relevant international code (010 from the UK, 011 from the US and Canada, 0011 from Australia, 00 from New Zealand and 16 from the Republic of Ireland), and followed by the number you require in Seychelles. To call home from Seychelles, dial the international access code (0), then the country code (44 for the UK, 1 for the US and Canada, 61 for Australia, 64 for New Zealand and 353 for the Republic of Ireland), and the area code (omitting the first digit) and the subscriber's number.

Useful numbers

Telegrams	13
Operator	18
Tourist Office	25335
Marine Charter	22126
Weather Forecast	73377
Taxis	23895

Time

Seychelles is four hours ahead of Greenwich Mean Time (three hours ahead of British Summer Time); 9–15 hours ahead of US time, 7½–13 hours ahead of Canadian time; 4–6 hours behind Australian time; and 8 hours behind New Zealand time.

Tipping

Hotels and restaurants add 10 per cent service charge to your account. Tipping is not expected other than in hotels frequented by package tours.

Elsewhere your small change is graciously accepted. Give porters SR2 per case.

Toilets

Mahé is not greatly blessed with public WCs and it is quite acceptable to use hotel facilities. In Victoria WCs are found in the arcade off the Pirate's Arms, at Marine Charter, the Yacht Club, behind the taxi-rank on Freedom Square and the Botanical Gardens. There is another in the Tea Tavern on the Sans Souci Road to Port Glaud. Most WCs are clean and supplied with paper.

Tourist Offices

There is a tourist information desk run by the National Travel Agency before Immigration at Mahé International Airport.

The head office of the Seychelles Tourist Office in Victoria has useful brochures and information sheets.

Address: Independence House, PO Box 92, Victoria, Mahé (tel: 25333).

STO Offices Overseas

UK: 2nd floor, Eros House, 111 Baker Street, London W1M 1FE (tel: (071) 224 1670).

US: c/o Mr M Morengo, Seychelles Mission to the UN, 820 Second Avenue, Suite 927, New York, NY10017 (tel: (212) 687 9766).

Travel Agencies

Interisland hotel bookings, car-rental, excursions, island travel, transfers, etc are made by three major agents with head offices in Mahé. Service is slick, guides are professional, friendly and well-groomed. Setting the style is Travel Services Seychelles (TSS) whose representatives wear smart blue uniforms with blue and green striped shirts. Competition is keen but TSS, Mason's and National Travel Agency (NTA) all help each other.

While not cheap, local excursions represent good value. The all day boat-trip to Sainte Anne Marine National Park includes transfers, glass-bottom boat, lunch including a drink and snorkelling.

A package-tour inclusive of air-fare and full board is the best way to visit Île Denis and Bird Island. Day charters to Frégate are popular.

Special bonuses are offered. Book any two excursions with TSS and you are eligible for an annual draw. The prize is a free return flight to Seychelles, two weeks at a hotel of your choice, transfers and SR1,000 spending money.

National Travel Agency: PO Box 611, Kingsgate House, Victoria, Mahé (tel: 24900). Location opposite the Tourist Office on Independence Avenue.
On Praslin – tel: 33223.
Mason's Travel: PO Box 459, Victoria, Mahé (tel: 22642). On Praslin – tel: 33211.
Travel Services Seychelles: PO Box 356, Victoria, Mahé, (tel: 22414). Located in Victoria House, State House Avenue. On Praslin – tel: 33438.
Bunson's Travel: IATA Agency, ticketing office, PO Box 336, Victoria, Mahé (tel: 22682). Located on Revolution Avenue, Victoria.

LANGUAGE

All educated Seychellois are bilingual in English and French which are official languages, and a knowledge of both is ideal. It may also be helpful to know at least a few words of Creole, also an official language. A somewhat sing-song derivative of French, it is spoken throughout the islands – and is also now used for written literature. There are no clear rules for speaking Creole except to enunciate clearly, placing emphasis on vowel sounds.

Useful Phrases
hello Alo
goodbye orevwar
how are you? comman sava?
yes wi
no non

Seychelloises have great style

LANGUAGE

I don't know mon pa konnen
I'm fine mon bien
I am unwell mon pa bien
I understand mon konpran
do you speak English?
eski ou koz Anglay?
how much is? konbien sa?
do you have? eski ou annan?
what is this...? ki si sa, sa...?
where is the WC?
kote kabinen i ete?
too much tro boukou
too little tro ti gin
too far tro lwen
not enough pa ase
too hot tro show
too cold tro fray
what is your name?
ki mannyer ou appel?
can you tell me?
eski ou kapab dir mwan?
what is the way to . . . ?
kote semen pou al . . . ?
turn left vir a gos
turn right vir a drwat
ahead devan
stop here aret isi
today ozordi
tomorrow demen
yesterday yer
what time does the plane
leave, please?
keler avyon i kite, silvouple?
is this our coach? sa nou bis?
where is the bank? ol i labank?
what is the time? keler i ete?
can I use the telephone?
mon kapab servi telefonn?
what time does the bar close?
keler bar i femen?

Places
airport erport
beach lanse
bus station stasyon bis
bookshop laboutik liv
ferry terminal terminal bato
church legliz
harbour lasose

hospital lopital
hotel lotel
island zil
museum mize
post office lapos
taxi-rank ran taksi/stenn

Foods, Fruits and Spices
Vegetables:
aubergine brenzel
bean zariko
cucumber konkom
pepper/pimento gro pimam
potato pom deter
pumpkin zironmon
mushroom sanpinyon
onion zonnyon
tomato tomat/pom damour

Fruits:
banana bannann
breadfruit friyapen
coconut coco
custard-apple zat
guava gouyav
lemon limon
melon melon
mango mang
papaya papay

Other Foods and Spices:
coffee kafe
chicken poul
cinnamon kannel
cloves zerof
crab krab
eggs dizef
fish pwason
ginger zenzam
octopus zourit
pork lavyann koson
prawn kanmaron
pepper dipwav
rice diri
salt disel
squid zourit vov
sugar disik
swordfish pwason sab
tea di tee

INDEX

The Automobile Association would like to thank the following photographers and libraries for their assistance in the preparation of this book:

CHRISTINE OSBORNE who took all the photographs in this book not listed below (AA PHOTO LIBRARY)

INTERNATIONAL PHOTOBANK Cover Mahé

NATURE PHOTOGRAPHERS LTD 56/7 Coco-de-mer palms (A J Watson), 61 White-tailed tropicbird (M E Gore), 63 Sooty tern colony (A J Watson), 83 Mahé coast (S C Bisserott), 85 Red headed fody (P Roberts), 88 Pitcher plant (S C Bisserott), 92 Grt Frigatebird (W S Paton).